no lex 11/3/12

MAO ZEDONG

MAO ZEDONG

Hedda Garza

CHELSEA HOUSE PUBLISHERS
NEW YORK
NEW HAVEN   PHILADELPHIA

EDITOR-IN-CHIEF: Nancy Toff
EXECUTIVE EDITOR: Remmel T. Nunn
MANAGING EDITOR: Karyn Gullen Browne
COPY CHIEF: Juliann Barbato
PICTURE EDITOR: Adrian G. Allen
ART DIRECTOR: Giannella Garrett
MANUFACTURING MANAGER: Gerald Levine

Staff for MAO ZEDONG:

SENIOR EDITOR: John W. Selfridge
ASSISTANT EDITOR: Sean Dolan
COPY EDITOR: James Guiry
EDITORIAL ASSISTANT: Sean Ginty
ASSOCIATE PICTURE EDITOR: Juliette Dickstein
PICTURE RESEARCHER: Karen Herman
SENIOR DESIGNER: David Murray
ASSISTANT DESIGNER: Jill Goldreyer
PRODUCTION COORDINATOR: Joseph Romano
COVER ILLUSTRATION: © Richard Leonard

CREATIVE DIRECTOR: Harold Steinberg

Frontispiece courtesy of The Bettmann Archive

First Printing

1 3 5 7 9 8 6 4 2

Library of Congress Cataloging in Publication Data

Garza, Hedda, MAO ZEDONG

(World leaders past & present)
1. Mao, Tse–tung, 1893–1976—Juvenile literature.
2. Heads of state—China—Biography—Juvenile literature.
[1. Mao, Tse–tung, 1893–1976. 2. Heads of
state] I. Title. II. Series: World leaders past & present.
DS778.M3G39   1988   951.05′.092′4 [E] [92] 87-18331

ISBN 0-87754-564-2

Contents

WORLD LEADERS   PAST & PRESENT

John Adams
John Quincy Adams
Konrad Adenauer
Alexander the Great
Salvador Allende
Marc Antony
Corazon Aquino
Yasir Arafat
King Arthur
Hafez al-Assad
Kemal Atatürk
Attila
Clement Attlee
Augustus Caesar
Menachem Begin
David Ben-Gurion
Otto von Bismarck
Léon Blum
Simon Bolívar
Cesare Borgia
Willy Brandt
Leonid Brezhnev
Julius Caesar
John Calvin
Jimmy Carter
Fidel Castro
Catherine the Great
Charlemagne
Chiang Kai-Shek
Winston Churchill
Georges Clemenceau
Cleopatra
Constantine the Great
Hernán Cortés
Oliver Cromwell
Georges-Jacques
  Danton
Jefferson Davis
Moshe Dayan
Charles de Gaulle
Eamon De Valera
Eugene Debs
Deng Xiaoping
Benjamin Disraeli
Alexander Dubček
François & Jean-Claude
  Duvalier
Dwight Eisenhower
Eleanor of Aquitaine
Elizabeth I
Faisal
Ferdinand & Isabella
Francisco Franco
Benjamin Franklin

Frederick the Great
Indira Gandhi
Mohandas Gandhi
Giuseppe Garibaldi
Amin & Bashir Gemayel
Genghis Khan
William Gladstone
Mikhail Gorbachev
Ulysses S. Grant
Ernesto "Che" Guevara
Tenzin Gyatso
Alexander Hamilton
Dag Hammarskjöld
Henry viii
Henry of Navarre
Paul von Hindenburg
Hirohito
Adolf Hitler
Ho Chi Minh
King Hussein
Ivan the Terrible
Andrew Jackson
James i
Wojciech Jaruzelski
Thomas Jefferson
Joan of Arc
Pope John xxiii
Pope John Paul ii
Lyndon Johnson
Benito Juárez
John Kennedy
Robert Kennedy
Jomo Kenyatta
Ayatollah Khomeini
Nikita Khrushchev
Kim Il Sung
Martin Luther King, Jr.
Henry Kissinger
Kublai Khan
Lafayette
Robert E. Lee
Vladimir Lenin
Abraham Lincoln
David Lloyd George
Louis xiv
Martin Luther
Judas Maccabeus
James Madison
Nelson & Winnie
  Mandela
Mao Zedong
Ferdinand Marcos
George Marshall

Mary, Queen of Scots
Tomáš Masaryk
Golda Meir
Klemens von Metternich
James Monroe
Hosni Mubarak
Robert Mugabe
Benito Mussolini
Napoléon Bonaparte
Gamal Abdel Nasser
Jawaharlal Nehru
Nero
Nicholas II
Richard Nixon
Kwame Nkrumah
Daniel Ortega
Mohammed Reza Pahlavi
Thomas Paine
Charles Stewart
  Parnell
Pericles
Juan Perón
Peter the Great
Pol Pot
Muammar el-Qaddafi
Ronald Reagan
Cardinal Richelieu
Maximilien Robespierre
Eleanor Roosevelt
Franklin Roosevelt
Theodore Roosevelt
Anwar Sadat
Haile Selassie
Prince Sihanouk
Jan Smuts
Joseph Stalin
Sukarno
Sun Yat-sen
Tamerlane
Mother Teresa
Margaret Thatcher
Josip Broz Tito
Toussaint L'Ouverture
Leon Trotsky
Pierre Trudeau
Harry Truman
Queen Victoria
Lech Walesa
George Washington
Chaim Weizmann
Woodrow Wilson
Xerxes
Emiliano Zapata
Zhou Enlai

CHELSEA HOUSE PUBLISHERS

ON LEADERSHIP

Arthur M. Schlesinger, jr.

LEADERSHIP, it may be said, is really what makes the world go round. Love no doubt smooths the passage; but love is a private transaction between consenting adults. Leadership is a public transaction with history. The idea of leadership affirms the capacity of individuals to move, inspire, and mobilize masses of people so that they act together in pursuit of an end. Sometimes leadership serves good purposes, sometimes bad; but whether the end is benign or evil, great leaders are those men and women who leave their personal stamp on history.

Now, the very concept of leadership implies the proposition that individuals can make a difference. This proposition has never been universally accepted. From classical times to the present day, eminent thinkers have regarded individuals as no more than the agents and pawns of larger forces, whether the gods and goddesses of the ancient world or, in the modern era, race, class, nation, the dialectic, the will of the people, the spirit of the times, history itself. Against such forces, the individual dwindles into insignificance.

So contends the thesis of historical determinism. Tolstoy's great novel *War and Peace* offers a famous statement of the case. Why, Tolstoy asked, did millions of men in the Napoleonic Wars, denying their human feelings and their common sense, move back and forth across Europe slaughtering their fellows? "The war," Tolstoy answered, "was bound to happen simply because it was bound to happen." All prior history predetermined it. As for leaders, they, Tolstoy said, "are but the labels that serve to give a name to an end and, like labels, they have the least possible connection with the event." The greater the leader, "the more conspicuous the inevitability and the predestination of every act he commits." The leader, said Tolstoy, is "the slave of history."

Determinism takes many forms. Marxism is the determinism of class. Nazism the determinism of race. But the idea of men and women as the slaves of history runs athwart the deepest human instincts. Rigid determinism abolishes the idea of human freedom—

the assumption of free choice that underlies every move we make, every word we speak, every thought we think. It abolishes the idea of human responsibility, since it is manifestly unfair to reward or punish people for actions that are by definition beyond their control. No one can live consistently by any deterministic creed. The Marxist states prove this themselves by their extreme susceptibility to the cult of leadership.

More than that, history refutes the idea that individuals make no difference. In December 1931 a British politician crossing Park Avenue in New York City between 76th and 77th Streets around 10:30 P.M. looked in the wrong direction and was knocked down by an automobile—a moment, he later recalled, of a man aghast, a world aglare: "I do not understand why I was not broken like an eggshell or squashed like a gooseberry." Fourteen months later an American politician, sitting in an open car in Miami, Florida, was fired on by an assassin; the man beside him was hit. Those who believe that individuals make no difference to history might well ponder whether the next two decades would have been the same had Mario Constasino's car killed Winston Churchill in 1931 and Giuseppe Zangara's bullet killed Franklin Roosevelt in 1933. Suppose, in addition, that Adolf Hitler had been killed in the street fighting during the Munich *Putsch* of 1923 and that Lenin had died of typhus during World War I. What would the 20th century be like now?

For better or for worse, individuals do make a difference. "The notion that a people can run itself and its affairs anonymously," wrote the philosopher William James, "is now well known to be the silliest of absurdities. Mankind does nothing save through initiatives on the part of inventors, great or small, and imitation by the rest of us—these are the sole factors in human progress. Individuals of genius show the way, and set the patterns, which common people then adopt and follow."

Leadership, James suggests, means leadership in thought as well as in action. In the long run, leaders in thought may well make the greater difference to the world. But, as Woodrow Wilson once said, "Those only are leaders of men, in the general eye, who lead in action. . . . It is at their hands that new thought gets its translation into the crude language of deeds." Leaders in thought often invent in solitude and obscurity, leaving to later generations the tasks of imitation. Leaders in action—the leaders portrayed in this series—have to be effective in their own time.

And they cannot be effective by themselves. They must act in response to the rhythms of their age. Their genius must be adapted, in a phrase of William James's, "to the receptivities of the moment." Leaders are useless without followers. "There goes the mob," said the French politician hearing a clamor in the streets. "I am their leader. I must follow them." Great leaders turn the inchoate emotions of the mob to purposes of their own. They seize on the opportunities of their time, the hopes, fears, frustrations, crises, potentialities. They succeed when events have prepared the way for them, when the community is awaiting to be aroused, when they can provide the clarifying and organizing ideas. Leadership ignites the circuit between the individual and the mass and thereby alters history.

It may alter history for better or for worse. Leaders have been responsible for the most extravagant follies and most monstrous crimes that have beset suffering humanity. They have also been vital in such gains as humanity has made in individual freedom, religious and racial tolerance, social justice, and respect for human rights.

There is no sure way to tell in advance who is going to lead for good and who for evil. But a glance at the gallery of men and women in *World Leaders—Past and Present* suggests some useful tests.

One test is this: Do leaders lead by force or by persuasion? By command or by consent? Through most of history leadership was exercised by the divine right of authority. The duty of followers was to defer and to obey. "Theirs not to reason why / Theirs but to do and die." On occasion, as with the so-called enlightened despots of the 18th century in Europe, absolutist leadership was animated by humane purposes. More often, absolutism nourished the passion for domination, land, gold, and conquest and resulted in tyranny.

The great revolution of modern times has been the revolution of equality. The idea that all people should be equal in their legal condition has undermined the old structure of authority, hierarchy, and deference. The revolution of equality has had two contrary effects on the nature of leadership. For equality, as Alexis de Tocqueville pointed out in his great study *Democracy in America,* might mean equality in servitude as well as equality in freedom.

"I know of only two methods of establishing equality in the political world," Tocqueville wrote. "Rights must be given to every citizen, or none at all to anyone . . . save one, who is the master of all." There was no middle ground "between the sovereignty of all and the absolute power of one man." In his astonishing prediction of 20th-century totalitarian dictatorship, Tocqueville explained how the revolution of equality could lead to the *"Führerprinzip"* and more terrible absolutism than the world had ever known.

But when rights are given to every citizen and the sovereignty of all is established, the problem of leadership takes a new form, becomes more exacting than ever before. It is easy to issue commands and enforce them by the rope and the stake, the concentration camp and the *gulag.* It is much harder to use argument and achievement to overcome opposition and win consent. The Founding Fathers of the United States understood the difficulty. They believed that history had given them the opportunity to decide, as Alexander Hamilton wrote in the first Federalist Paper, whether men are indeed capable of basing government on "reflection and choice, or whether they are forever destined to depend . . . on accident and force."

Government by reflection and choice called for a new style of leadership and a new quality of followership. It required leaders to be responsive to popular concerns, and it required followers to be active and informed participants in the process. Democracy does not eliminate emotion from politics; sometimes it fosters demagoguery; but it is confident that, as the greatest of democratic leaders put it, you cannot fool all of the people all of the time. It measures leadership by results and retires those who overreach or falter or fail.

It is true that in the long run despots are measured by results too. But they can postpone the day of judgment, sometimes indefinitely, and in the meantime they can do infinite harm. It is also true that democracy is no guarantee of virtue and intelligence in government, for the voice of the people is not necessarily the voice of God. But democracy, by assuring the right of opposition, offers built-in resistance to the evils inherent in absolutism. As the theologian Reinhold Niebuhr summed it up, "Man's capacity for justice makes democracy possible, but man's inclination to injustice makes democracy necessary."

A second test for leadership is the end for which power is sought. When leaders have as their goal the supremacy of a master race or the promotion of totalitarian revolution or the acquisition and exploitation of colonies or the protection of greed and privilege or the preservation of personal power, it is likely that their leadership will do little to advance the cause of humanity. When their goal is the abolition of slavery, the liberation of women, the enlargement of opportunity for the poor and powerless, the extension of equal rights to racial minorities, the defense of the freedoms of expression and opposition, it is likely that their leadership will increase the sum of human liberty and welfare.

Leaders have done great harm to the world. They have also conferred great benefits. You will find both sorts in this series. Even "good" leaders must be regarded with a certain wariness. Leaders are not demigods; they put on their trousers one leg after another just like ordinary mortals. No leader is infallible, and every leader needs to be reminded of this at regular intervals. Irreverence irritates leaders but is their salvation. Unquestioning submission corrupts leaders and demeans followers. Making a cult of a leader is always a mistake. Fortunately hero worship generates its own antidote. "Every hero," said Emerson, "becomes a bore at last."

The signal benefit the great leaders confer is to embolden the rest of us to live according to our own best selves, to be active, insistent, and resolute in affirming our own sense of things. For great leaders attest to the reality of human freedom against the supposed inevitabilities of history. And they attest to the wisdom and power that may lie within the most unlikely of us, which is why Abraham Lincoln remains the supreme example of great leadership. A great leader, said Emerson, exhibits new possibilities to all humanity. "We feed on genius. . . . Great men exist that there may be greater men."

Great leaders, in short, justify themselves by emancipating and empowering their followers. So humanity struggles to master its destiny, remembering with Alexis de Tocqueville: "It is true that around every man a fatal circle is traced beyond which he cannot pass; but within the wide verge of that circle he is powerful and free; as it is with man, so with communities."

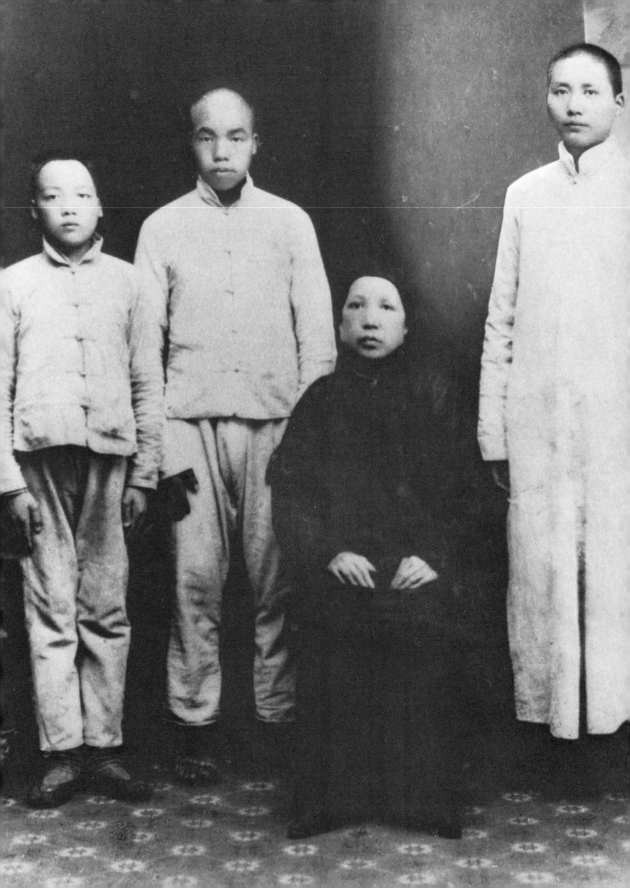

1

The Enemy Advances

Four hundred soldiers were not many with which to make a revolution, especially not in a country of more than 400 million people, but they were all that remained. Worse, these 400 were soldiers in name only; they were the ragtag survivors of the ill-fated Autumn Harvest Uprising in Hunan province — miners, peasants, and Guomindang deserters. Mao Zedong had led them 300 miles to the southeast, to the mountains of Jinggangshan, a region along the border of Hunan and Jiangxi provinces.

It was October 1927. Mao had worked since 1920 to foment a communist revolution as a solution to China's problems. In 1924, at the direction of the Soviet Union, the world's only communist state and leader of the world communist movement, the CCP (Chinese Communist party) had allied itself with the *Guomindang*, or Nationalist party, of Sun Yat-sen, which was also fighting to overthrow China's military government. The alliance had been broken in April 1927, when Chiang Kai-shek, Sun's succes-

Weapons are an important factor in war, but not the decisive factor; it is people, not things, that are decisive. The contest of strength is not only a contest of human power and morale. Military and economic power is necessarily wielded by people.
—MAO ZEDONG

Mao Zedong as a young man of 26 (far right), with his mother, Wen Chimei, and brothers Zetan (far left) and Zemin. Mao spent his childhood in rebellion against the discipline of his father, who required unquestioning obedience and expected Mao to spend long hours working the family land.

Shaoshan, where Mao was born and grew up, was a small village in Hunan province. Most of its inhabitants were peasants who lived barely above subsistence level, growing rice and jute on small plots of land rented from absentee landlords.

sor, brutally massacred his Communist supporters in Shanghai. The Communists were routed in other cities as well and purged from their Guomindang positions. In the summer of that year the Communists had planned their own offensives, rebellions aimed at urban and rural targets, timed to coincide with the autumn harvest. Mao was directed to lead the uprising in Hunan, in south-central China. In contrast with doctrinaire communist ideology, which held that the urban laborers would lead a workers' revolution, Mao had emphasized to the CCP leadership the revolutionary potential of China's impoverished peasantry. He believed in the summer of 1927 that the time for China's own "October Revolution" (as Russia's 1917 communist revolution was known) was at hand and assured the leadership that Hunan's peasantry and the workers of Changsha, Hunan's largest city, would rally to the Autumn Harvest Uprising. Mao promised the leadership that 100,000 peasants would take part.

Mao was able to put together only 4 motley regiments, totaling approximately 5,000 men. The regiments were given the grandiloquent name of the First Workers' and Peasants' Revolutionary Army. The two regiments of Guomindang deserters fought each other, the Changsha workers ignored the uprising, and the remaining two regiments were badly defeated by Chiang's troops. Mao himself was captured and had to escape to avoid execution.

To Jinggangshan in November came word that the CCP leadership held Mao responsible for the failure of the uprising in Hunan. He was accused of "military opportunism, inadequate peasant mobilization, collaboration with bandits, and failure to obey [party] directives" and was dismissed from the party's central committee. The CCP called him "a deserter abandoning the masses."

Mao was unmoved. It had been plain to him for some time that the party leadership had made serious mistakes, showing little interest in Mao's theories about the peasantry and rejecting his suggestion that the Communists establish rural bases from which to carry out the revolution. Though now little more than a discredited military leader in the eyes of the CCP, Mao was still determined to carry out the revolution. He no doubt pondered his favorite quotation from the 4th-century B.C. ethical philosopher Mencius: "When Heaven is about to confer a great office on any man, it first exercises his mind with suffering, and his sinews and bones with toil. It exposes his body to hunger and subjects him to extreme poverty. It confounds his undertakings. By all these methods it stimulates his mind, hardens his nature, and supplies his incompetencies."

Isolated for centuries, China remained untouched by western technological innovations that accompanied industrialization in Europe and the New World. Even into the early 20th century, Chinese peasants irrigated their fields with wooden foot paddles, as they had for centuries.

On the way to Jinggangshan, Mao had promised his 400 troops democracy, free speech, and party control over officers. Thus was born the Red Army, whose skill, fortitude, patriotism, and effectiveness as a fighting force over the next two decades would make them legendary. At Jinggangshan Mao perfected his theories. It would be some time before the Communists would be strong enough to engage the Nationalists in pitched battles. The Communists, Mao believed, would have to fight a guerrilla war. He encapsulated the new military policy in four brief sentences:

> The enemy advances, we retreat.
> The enemy halts and encamps, we harass.
> The enemy seeks to avoid battle, we attack.
> The enemy retreats, we pursue.

Likewise, the army was given "three rules of discipline" and "six points of attention," designed both to ensure discipline and win the support of the peasantry. According to the rules of discipline, a soldier was never to take a single needle or thread from the people, was to obey all orders, and was to turn in everything that was captured. The points for attention required a soldier to put back doors taken down to serve as beds and straw taken for bedding, speak politely, pay for everything consumed or damaged, and return everything borrowed.

The mandarins, imperial China's bureaucrats and administrators, had to pass state examinations on their knowledge of the Chinese classics and Confucian philosophy in order to obtain their positions. The mandarins disdained physical labor and constituted an elite social class within China.

Jinggangshan encompassed approximately 5,400 square miles. Red Army troops guarded all paths through the mountains, making Mao's stronghold virtually impregnable. Mao established a hospital and bedding and clothing workshops. Malnourishment and deaths from exposure due to inadequate clothing were constant problems, but the Red Army never resorted to looting.

Soon the Red Army was joined by bandit leaders who pledged that their men would obey Mao's rules. The Communist general Zhu De Chu Teh and the brilliant young officer Lin Biao came to Jinggangshan, bringing reinforcements. As their numbers increased, the Communists formed a people's government at Chaling, establishing a legislative body of workers, peasants, and soldiers. The Communists steadily expanded their influence, winning the support of the peasants through their promises of land redistribution and the creation of an egalitarian state controlled by the peasants and the workers.

By 1929 Mao felt his Red Army had sufficient strength to come down out of Jinggangshan and establish itself in Jiangxi. In an article he wrote in October of that year, Mao stated that Jinggangshan, where the Communists were able to establish and exercise political power in an area encircled by opposition forces, was a "phenomenon which has never occurred anywhere else in the world." There would be 20 years of fighting before the Communists would triumph, but after Jinggangshan Mao had no doubts that his methods would work in China. When, in 1934, poor leadership again brought the Communists to the brink of defeat by the Nationalists, it was Mao who emerged as the party's supreme political and military leader.

Mao Zedong was born on December 26, 1893, in Shaoshan, a village in Hunan, which is one of China's most important farming regions. The people of the province have long enjoyed great renown throughout all China for their industriousness,

The 6th-century B.C. philosopher Confucius emphasized an ordered society based on strictly defined social relationships. He taught, for example, that the duty owed a father by his son was similar to that owed a ruler by his subjects. Confucian thought permeates much of Chinese culture.

their sense of community, and their fiery temperament. The Hunanese are also legendary for their courage: "China can be conquered," goes an old Chinese saying, "only when every Hunanese is dead."

Mao's grandfather had settled in Shaoshan in the 1870s. In 1878 he built a modest, one-room farmhouse. Mao's father, Mao Jenshen, started working in the fields when he reached the age of eight. After a few bad harvests, the landlord took away the land, and at age 16 Mao Jenshen joined the imperial army to help pay his father's crushing debt. When Mao Jenshen returned home, his father was able to buy back half an acre from the landlord. A marriage was then arranged for Mao Jenshen according to Chinese custom. His bride was Wen Chimei, a woman from the nearby town of Xiangtan.

Many arranged marriages proved loveless, and Mao Jenshen and Wen Chimei's was no exception. Mao Jenshen expected his bride to work incredibly hard, to take care of him and his aging father, and to bear him many children in the shortest possible time. Wen spent her days cooking, washing, feeding livestock, dragging huge buckets of water from the well, hauling manure and straw to the fields, planting, hoeing, and harvesting. Her husband often beat her when he thought her work inadequate. Later, his children were subjected to the same treatment. Mao Jenshen was not, however, being consciously cruel, but was merely acting in accordance with Chinese tradition, which held that wives and children were little more than slaves.

Mao Zedong, the couple's first child, came into the world on a cot set up on the dirt floor of a tiny room next to the pigpen. Mao Jenshen was delighted at the birth of a boy. In five or six years, he would have a young, strong hand to work in the fields and an heir to all of the land he hoped to accumulate. More heirs and laborers were soon to come. When Mao was two, his brother Mao Zemin was born. When Mao was 12, the third and last son, Mao Zetan, joined the family. In 1906 a young girl cousin, Mao Zejian, came to live with the family.

Until he was six, young Zedong had a better life than most of the other children in the village. By the standards of the Hunan peasantry, Mao Jenshen had prospered. He had accumulated more than three acres of land, on which he grew more than enough rice to feed his family. The surplus was sold, and Mao Jenshen acted as a moneylender, at profitable repayment rates, to his neighbors. Mao never felt the pangs of hunger. While he was still too young to work, his father largely ignored him, and the child was left alone to search for crickets in the fields, or to accompany his mother up the steep trails to the tiny Buddhist temples that sat atop many of the nearby hills.

When Mao reached age six, he began working with his father in the fields. No matter how hard he worked, however, his father scolded him for laziness. From early childhood, Mao invariably argued back, a terrible offense in a traditional Chinese family.

Mao was sent to the village primary school when he was eight. He learned to read very quickly but found the official Confucian classics dull. He saw something wrong in what they preached: "Some labor with their minds," the books said, "and some labor with their strength. Those who labor with their minds govern others; those who labor with their strength are governed by others."

Mao was not alone in his discontent. At the dawn of the 20th century, China faced many problems. Foremost among them were extreme poverty, particularly among the peasantry, and domination by foreign powers. These were exacerbated by an outdated, out-of-touch monarchy, unwilling or unable to provide solutions.

As had been true for centuries, the great majority of Chinese were peasants, dependent on the land for their living. Most did not own their own property but rented or leased their small plots from landlords, to whom they were constantly in debt. The peasants labored to earn a subsistence living, growing just enough food (usually rice) to feed their families. Rent to the landlords was paid in rice. Very few

A Chinese opium den. Millions of Chinese became addicted to opium after British traders introduced it in large quantities in the early 19th century in order to subvert China's restrictions on trade with the West.

peasants were able to grow enough rice to sell for cash. China's population, 100 million in 1750, quadrupled in the next century. The land, already heavily worked, was unable to support the increase. The pressure to obtain land increased. Traditionally a man's sons divided his property at his death. This meant that family plots grew smaller and more insufficient. With millions of Chinese living at or below subsistence levels, the frequent crop failures and floods that plagued China meant mass starvation.

China had been ruled by a succession of imperial dynasties for more than 3,000 years. Since 1644 the Qing, or Manchu, dynasty had held power. China was administered by the *mandarins*, a highly educated class who filled national, regional, and local government posts. Their disdain for the physical labor that was the lot of most of their countrymen was symbolized by their practice of growing their fingernails long. The mandarins were versed in the precepts of Confucianism, named for the 6th-century B.C. philosopher Confucius. Confucianism was concerned primarily with ethics and morality and emphasized harmony and order and the mutual obligations of father and son and subject and sovereign. Its tenets were the basis for much of Chinese culture.

For centuries China had remained proudly isolated, calling itself the "Middle Kingdom" and regarding all foreigners as barbarians. Chinese civilization flourished while Europe was still in the Dark Ages. The Chinese invented paper, clocks, gunpowder, and printing, but by the mid-19th century traditional Chinese methods were insufficient to cope with the nation's problems. Isolated, China was bypassed by the technological innovations that transformed Europe. While Europe was undergoing the Industrial Revolution in the late 17th and 18th centuries, China stood still.

The newly industrialized European nations, busy expanding their wealth through foreign trade and the establishment of overseas colonies, were eager to exploit China's trade potential. While the Chinese initially resisted foreign trade incursions, for a time limiting it to the southern port of Guangzhou (Canton), the government's weakness was glaringly revealed by the Opium Wars, fought by Great Britain in the mid-1800s to force the Chinese to permit the sale of opium within the country. After the British victory, the European powers (and Japan) obtained numerous trade concessions from the compliant imperial government, carving China into "spheres of influence" under their respective flags. The "unequal treaties," as the concessions were known, were an affront to nationalist and patriotic Chinese.

By 1900 discontent was rampant. It had been manifested earlier, in 1850, by the Taiping Rebellion, led by Hung Xiuchan, who claimed divine inspiration and preached tenets of egalitarianism and collective ownership and decision making. The rebellion gained many adherents and was successful in many areas but was crushed in the early 1860s by imperial and European forces, at a total cost of 20 million lives. In 1900 a secret society known as the Boxers attacked foreign legations and missionary headquarters in Beijing (Peking) in the hope of driving the foreign influence from China, but the United States, Great Britain, France, Germany, Russia, and Italy put together an army that quickly quelled the Boxer Rebellion.

Mao's earliest escape from the drudgery of farm labor and the narrow confines of Shaoshan were adventure novels. Banned by the emperor, they were slipped into the village, hidden under the housewares in peddlers' carts. Mao managed to beg and borrow dog-eared copies of books with titles like *Revolt Against the Tang*, *Three Kingdoms*, *Travels in the West*, and *All Men Are Brothers* — stories of peasant revolts and outlaws who robbed the rich and gave to the poor, of love and rebellion.

There were, however, real events in distant places that would create far greater adventures for Mao than any of those portrayed in the novels he read. Hatred against all things foreign was intensifying throughout China. In exile in Japan, a young Chinese man by the name of Sun Yat-sen was form-

> *All political power comes from the barrel of a gun.*
> —MAO ZEDONG

21

China's great nationalist leader Sun Yat-sen worked to overthrow the Qing dynasty and hoped to establish a parliamentary democracy in China. Unlike the Qing emperors, Sun believed that China could benefit from the influence of Western ideas.

ing a revolutionary organization, the *Zhongguo Tong Meng Hui*, or Chinese United League, to overthrow the Qing dynasty. Sun envisioned a Chinese republic modeled on the parliamentary democracies of the West.

Shaoshan had no foreigners and no newspapers. Very little history was taught in the village school. It was probably months before news of the Boxer Rebellion or Sun's work reached Shaoshan, where Mao was already busy conducting his own small rebellions. When his teacher threatened to whip him for reading a novel in school, Mao ran out of the room and holed up in the hills. The villagers searched for him in vain. When he came back, he had won what he later called his "first strike" — his teacher never hit him again.

In 1906 famine and flood ravaged Hunan. In Changsha, Hunan's capital, peasants armed only with pitchforks broke into government offices and demanded the surplus rice in the landlords' warehouses. The authorities immediately rushed troops to the scene, and hundreds of peasants were beheaded. When Mao Jenshen voiced his approval of the government's action, Mao and his mother were shocked. Just weeks after the executions in Changsha, Mao's father's own small rice convoy was stopped and confiscated by hungry peasants. Mao Jenshen raged for hours, but his son loudly supported what the peasants had done.

That same year the elder Mao declared that his son was now sufficiently educated and ought to be ready for full-time work. Mao, who longed to continue his education, became despondent. It was also at around this time that Mao's father arranged for him to marry. Mao's bride was 19, and Mao's father looked forward to the extra labor she could provide. The children the young couple were sure to have would also be welcome in the fields in a few years' time. Mao had other ideas. He rejected his bride and refused to live with her. He said later that he never considered her to be his wife. The quarrels between Mao and his father grew more bitter, and in later years Mao was to say that he hated him.

Wanting more than anything to learn about the world outside, Mao left home without his father's permission and traveled to Xiangtan, where he stayed with a law student who had offered to tutor him. At his friend's house Mao read as much as he wanted — history books, essays, novels. He learned about real-life warriors — Taiping rebels and Boxers. One book, *Words of Warning*, made a lasting impression on him. Its subtitle was *On China's Danger of Being Dismembered by Foreign Powers*.

After six months, Mao's father demanded that he return home. Four years and many quarrels later, the elder Mao tried to apprentice his son to a rice merchant in Xiangtan, but Mao wanted to attend high school in the nearby town of Xiangxiang instead. His father refused even to consider the idea, asserting that there was no money to pay for a farmhand to replace his son.

Mao then borrowed money from his mother's relatives and presented his father with the then considerable sum of $12, a full year's wages for a farmhand. Then, having embraced his mother and without saying good-bye to his father, Mao hoisted his knapsack onto his shoulder and trudged the 15 miles to Xiangxiang. He would never again live in the same house as his father.

2
Revolution Betrayed

Mao arrived at the Dongshan Higher Primary School in Xiangxiang during the noon recess. Finely dressed students, most of them the sons of landlords or well-off peasants, were milling in the courtyard. It amused them to see this six-foot-tall peasant boy, dressed in dusty, faded pants and a tattered jacket, gazing in awe at their school and asking for the headmaster. Mao, however, stood his ground. His composure and bearing greatly impressed the headmaster, who agreed to admit Mao to the school for a five-month-long trial period.

Within a few weeks, Mao was winning praise from his teachers. He also earned the grudging respect of the other boys, but he was still dissatisfied. The texts he had to read were the same old Confucian classics that he had encountered at his previous school. Only one teacher, a man whom the boys called "False Pigtail," gave Mao a glimpse of modern ideas. False Pigtail had cut off his braid, the traditional sign of subservience to the emperor, when he was in Japan, and had become a supporter of Sun Yat-sen. Now, to keep his job, he wore a false braid.

A revolution does not march a straight line. It wanders where it can, retreats before superior forces, advances wherever it has room, attacks whenever the enemy retreats or bluffs and, above all, is possessed of enormous patience.
—MAO ZEDONG

Traditional Chinese men wore a long pigtail as a badge of their subservience to the emperor. The 18-year-old Mao, a dedicated follower of Sun Yat-sen and other progressive reformers, had his pigtail cut off, a gesture symbolic of his rebellion against outmoded tradition and China's feudal heritage.

Mao said that as a young man his ideas were a "curious mixture" of liberalism, democratic reformism, and utopian socialism. He received an education steeped in the Chinese classics and Confucianism, but on his own he read the works of such important Western thinkers as John Stuart Mill, Jean Jacques Rousseau, and Adam Smith.

False Pigtail explained Sun Yat-sen's theories to Mao. Sun believed that there would have to be a new China, a China conforming to Western ideas, with a strong central government ruling over a unified, industrialized nation through a democratically elected parliament. Mao borrowed a book, *Great Heroes of the Western World*, from his new friend. In it he read about George Washington, Abraham Lincoln, and the famous French soldier and statesman Napoleon. He decided that Sun Yat-sen was the George Washington of China and that the foreigners in China were the equivalent of the British in colonial America.

Mao soon became restless at the Dongshan school and decided to transfer to the secondary school at Changsha, a modern, more progressive institution. His mother again came to his rescue, this time with the last of her secret savings. Mao passed the entrance examination for the new school without difficulty and arrived in Changsha in the fall of 1911. Mao had never been in a city before, and the sight of huge mansions, elegant temples, and handsome parks overwhelmed him at first. Soon after arriving, Mao bought his first newspaper, *Strength of the People*, an official publication of Sun Yat-sen's Nationalist movement.

Political debate was a favorite pastime of the students at Xiangxiang Middle School, just as Mao had hoped would be the case. Many students supported Sun Yat-sen's ideas and dreamed of revolution. Mao soon wrote his first article, which called for a coalition between Sun Yat-sen and two other leading reformers, Kang Youwei and Liang Qichao. Mao was now in full-scale rebellion against the "Chinese way," and he and one of his friends cut off their pigtails and then forcibly gave haircuts to 10 other boys who had reneged on their promises to dispose of their badges of subservience.

In October 1911 Sun Yat-sen's revolution broke out at Wuhan, a major industrial center in Hubei province. The Qing regime had collapsed in that city when the emperor's soldiers and sailors joined the revolutionaries. A few days later, revolutionary forces arrived at Changsha. Mao stood on a hill and watched a brief battle at the city gates. In a matter of hours, the government troops were in retreat. Republican soldiers swept through the city, most of them, to Mao's amazement and delight, in laborers' clothes. At last, he thought, the common people were in charge. Mao believed that China would be transformed, that the revolution would eliminate the poverty and misery that had plagued the majority of the Chinese for so long. The 2,000-year-old monarchy had been swept away. Mao joined the revolutionary army in Changsha.

Disillusionment came quickly, and after six months Mao left the army. The revolutionaries organized a new government, but the concerns of the warlords, landlords, and businessmen who had backed Sun in his struggle against the ruling dynasty differed from those of the poor peasants and workers. In Changsha, two popular leaders of the peasant societies were murdered, and it was rumored that military colleagues of Sun Yat-sen had ordered the killings. Mao began to realize that the generals who had joined in the coalition with Sun Yat-sen held the real power.

Sun Yat-sen, who had been living in exile when the revolution began, returned to become provisional president of the Chinese republic. A little more than one month later, on February 12, 1912,

During his student days, Mao lived in this building in the Hunan city of Changsha. Mao left home, borrowed money, and endured hardship and poverty in order to obtain an education, but later, as China's leader, he downplayed its importance for young people.

Mao studied to be a teacher at Changsha's First Normal School from 1913 to 1918. He worked intermittently as an educator in Hunan in the early 1920s. Years later, he would encourage the people to think of him as the "Great Teacher."

he dissolved his government in Nanjing and reluctantly resigned the presidency in favor of Yuan Shikai, an important military leader who had secured the support of the foreign powers.

All of Sun Yat-sen's hopes and dreams had come to nothing. The republic's first parliament proved to be a singularly hollow institution, without power or prestige. Sun's new party, the Guomindang, or Nationalist party, opposed Yuan and won a majority in the National Assembly, but Yuan maintained power, often using brutal methods, such as the assassination of Song Jiaoren, one of the Guomindang's leaders, to do so.

In the spring of 1912 Mao decided to study on his own for six months. He spent most of his waking hours at the Hunan Provincial Library in Changsha. He was the first person to enter in the morning and the last to leave at night. His father once again refused to give him money, so Mao lodged at a cheap boardinghouse where students, vagrants, and soldiers slept on the floor. His diet consisted of little more than a few rice cakes each day, and he grew terribly gaunt. In later years he often referred to his personal initiative to improve himself as the best part of his education. He had been "like an ox let loose in a vegetable garden," reading until he could see no more.

Early in 1913 Mao decided to enroll at Changsha's teachers' training school, called the First Normal School, where he was given free tuition. There were other scholarship students there, too, poor young men from peasant and worker families, and he made some close friends.

In the late summer of that year the Nationalist revolution gasped its last breath. The Guomindang attempted a coup and several of the southern provinces declared their independence, but Yuan Shikai's forces finally were victorious. Yuan was not committed to parliamentary government or reform; with the defeat of his main rivals, he set about consolidating his own power. By 1915 he was preparing to declare himself emperor. In the provinces military governors were given a free hand in exchange for not placing too many demands on the central government. Individuals formed their own armies and wrung food and money from the countryside and peasantry. These warlords divided China into hundreds of military fiefdoms, a situation that became worse after the death of Yuan Shikai in 1916.

In August 1914 international attention suddenly became focused on events in Europe. Austria-Hungary had declared war on Serbia on July 28, and Serbia's ally Russia mobilized its forces along the German and Austrian frontiers on July 29. Germany then declared war on Russia on August 1 and on Russia's ally France on August 3. When Germany violated Belgian neutrality by invading that country, Britain, which was allied with Belgium, declared war on Germany.

The outbreak of hostilities between the major colonial powers had immediate repercussions for China, whose technical neutrality in the confict did not protect her from its effects. Japan, which had concluded an alliance with Britain before the war began, declared war on Germany on August 23 and immediately captured Germany's holdings in the Shandong Peninsula in northeastern China, occupying almost half the province.

The occupation of Shandong was soon revealed to have been but the first action in a wider Japanese

The Qing dynasty was overthrown in 1911, but the revolution was undermined by the ascension to power of military commander Yuan Shikai (pictured), who became China's first president. Yuan's primary concern was maintaining himself in power, and his dictatorial methods quickly brought the Chinese republic to an end.

effort to compromise Chinese sovereignty. In January 1915 Japanese diplomats visited Yuan Shikai and presented him with a list of demands, known as the "Twenty-one Demands," that reflected their government's determination to make Japan the leading imperialist power in China. In addition to demanding the extension of its existing privileges in China, Japan ordered Yuan to appoint Japanese political, military, and financial advisers to positions in China's central government.

When the substance of the Japanese demands was leaked to the press, China was convulsed by an upsurge of anti-Japanese feeling. China's diplomats had little difficulty persuading Japan's allies among the foreign powers to put pressure on the Japanese government, which duly modified its position. The agreement reached between the Chinese and Japanese governments on May 9, 1915, did, however, allow Japan some extension of commercial privileges. Many Chinese felt that China had conceded too much.

Although his political ideas were still largely unformed, Mao had become a popular student leader, winning the most votes in an election for representatives to the student union. Earlier he had organized fellow students to protest the school's inefficient, excessively bureaucratic administration. Now he convinced them to demonstrate against the Twenty-one Demands and to inform the workers of Changsha about Japan's aggressive policies.

China came no closer to democracy during Mao's years at the First Normal School. Yuan Shikai had abolished the National Assembly in 1914. Foreign interests still had the upper hand. Following Yuan Shikai's death in June 1916, Sun Yat-sen returned to China from Japan. By July 1917 there were two competing governments. The warlord Duan Qirui and his colleagues governed from Beijing, while Sun and a group of warlords friendly to his cause ruled parts of southern China from Guangzhou.

In the summer of 1917 Mao and a friend named Emi Xiao walked 300 miles across Hunan province,

Mao in his mid-twenties. The abuses of power by Yuan Shikai and the warlord governments that controlled China after his death in 1916 left Mao pessimistic about the prospects for progressive reform of Chinese society.

begging for food, talking to the peasants, and taking notes on everything they learned. When Mao and his friend returned to Changsha in the fall, Mao founded the New People's Study Society, calling for "reform of China and the world and against prostitution, opium, gambling, drinking, and corruption." The rules of the society forbade romantic involvements on the ground that they represented an infringement of the rights of women. Vigorous physical training and intense discussion of politics took up all the spare time of the members of the society. They plunged into icy lakes in the middle of winter and hiked until their feet were swollen and blistered. Despite the stringent requirements, by 1919 the group had 80 members and supporters drawn from Changsha's intellectuals and factory workers.

At the end of 1917 news of the Russian Revolution reached China. Before the Revolution, Russia had been a backward, agrarian nation ruled by an autocratic tsar. In November 1917 Vladimir Ilyich

Lenin and his Bolshevik party seized power from the provisional government and declared Russia a socialist state.

Lenin was the foremost intellectual disciple of Karl Marx, the 19th-century German economic, social, and political philosopher, whose writings form the basis of modern communist thought. Marx believed that capitalism — the economic system based on private enterprise — contains the seeds of its own destruction in that it inevitably concentrates ownership of property and the productive assets of a society in the hands of a small, elite class Marx called the *bourgeoisie*. The inequalities and injustices that result lead to capitalism's replacement by communism, a socioeconomic order in which private property has been abolished and people live in harmony and equality, without classes or other social divisions that necessitate the exercise of authority. According to the radical thinkers who built upon Marx's foundation, communism can be realized only following the creation of an intermediate order called socialism, in which the proletariat, or industrial working class, owns the means of production — the land and the factories. Marx also held that the transition from capitalism to communism can be achieved only by revolution, that control of the means of production must be seized from the bourgeoisie because no bourgeois will give up his property willingly in the interests of equality. Given the inherent injustice of the capitalist system, Marx viewed both the clash between the bourgeoisie and proletariat and the eventual triumph of communism as inevitable.

Mao and his colleagues in the New People's Study Society found the news from Russia fascinating. They discussed it at length, trying to work out whether what had happened in Russia might hold some lessons for Chinese radicals. Marx himself would have been surprised to learn that the first successful communist revolution took place in Russia, where democracy was untried and where the majority of the population were not industrial workers but peasants. Marx viewed advanced, industrial

The 19th-century German economist and political philosopher Karl Marx outlined what he saw as the inevitable triumph of communism over capitalism. With the success of the communist revolution in Russia in November 1917, Chinese reformers began to apply Marx's theories to conditions in their own country.

societies — capitalist democracies — as the natural forerunners of the communist order. Industrial workers in such democracies were generally better educated than their rural counterparts and could therefore more easily understand exactly how the capitalists exercised control over them. With a true understanding of the causes of their oppression, the workers would take the class war to its ultimate conclusion and overthrow the capitalists, achieving what Marx referred to as the "dictatorship of the proletariat."

In Marx's opinion, bringing about such changes in agrarian societies presented problems. He believed that the peasants were basically conservative and unreceptive to new ideas. The success of the Russian Revolution demonstrated that the communist order could be created in an agrarian country that lacked an urban, industrialized proletariat or a tradition of democracy. The example was not wasted on the Chinese radicals.

Russian revolutionary troops march under a banner reading "Communism" in Moscow in November 1917. Marx had predicted that communist revolutions would first take place in industrial democracies, but Russia was an autocracy with a predominantly agricultural economy.

3

Love and Marxism

In the fall of 1918 Mao received a letter from Professor Yang Zhangzhi, who had been his professor of ethics at the normal school. Yang, who was now teaching at Beijing University, urged him to broaden his horizons by enrolling in a work-study program in Paris, France. Mao had had no clear idea of what to do after graduation and found Yang's suggestion appealing. He traveled to Beijing to study French and earn money for the trip to Europe.

Yang helped Mao get a job in the periodicals section of the Beijing University Library. For eight dollars a month, Mao cleaned the rooms, put away books, and registered the names of borrowers. He tried to start discussions with the scholars who used the library, but most of them simply ignored him. Many of them were writers who belonged to the New Culture movement, which advocated democracy and equality for China, but they had no time to waste on a shabbily dressed Hunanese peasant with a southern dialect.

Learn from the masses, and then teach them.
—MAO ZEDONG

Mao's reading helped convince him that only a communist revolution could solve China's problems, although he was to break with orthodox Marxist theory in his insistence that China's peasantry constituted a potential revolutionary force. In July 1921 Mao was one of 12 founding members of the Chinese Communist party (CCP).

Li Dazhao was a scholar, writer, and republican reformer who, inspired by the Russian Revolution, wrote some of the first articles on Marxism to be published in China. He organized a Marxist study group in Beijing that Mao joined, and he later helped found the CCP in 1921.

Li Dazhao, Mao's superior at the library, was an exception. A scholar who admired the Russian Revolution, Li had translated some of Lenin's work into Chinese. Li believed that though the Russian Revolution had been made by the industrial proletariat, the Chinese revolution would be a peasant revolution. With another professor, Chen Duxiu, he ran a Marxist study group. He told its members that they should plan to work among the peasants: "Go to them, educate them, make them understand that they should demand their release from ignorance and misery and to be the masters of their own destiny." Li's ideas had a profound impact on Mao.

During his time in Beijing, Mao spent much of his spare time at Professor Yang's house. The professor's daughter, Yang Kaihui, was studying journalism at the university, and Mao began having long and earnest talks with her. Soon their relationship became very intimate, but they decided to postpone any decisions about their future until they knew each other better. It was also during this period that Mao became better acquainted with the plight of China's urban poor. He walked for hours in Beijing's working-class neighborhoods and was appalled by the contrast between the dismal hovels of the workers and the splendor of the old palace grounds.

When Professor Yang's work-study group was ready to embark on the journey to Europe, Mao decided not to go with them. He told them that he still had a great deal to learn about China. In addition, he had not saved much money and had found it very difficult to learn French. Mao's friends noted that Yang Kaihui also was staying in China. A few weeks after Yang's departure for France, Mao returned to Changsha, where he landed a part-time job teaching history at a primary school. He did not earn much, but he wanted time to continue his studies.

Early in 1919, China witnessed the greatest explosion of nationalist protest in its history. World War I had ended with Germany's defeat in November 1918, and representatives of the victorious Allied powers (France, Great Britain, the United States, and Italy) gathered in Paris in January 1919 for a conference that was intended to negotiate a peace settlement. China, which had entered the war on the Allied side in 1917, had great hopes that the conference would negotiate a just peace. President Woodrow Wilson of the United States had declared the "just settlement of all colonial claims" as one of the United States's war aims. Many Chinese interpreted this to mean that the peace treaty negotiated at Paris would end foreign domination of their nation.

In April 1919 the Allied powers formally endorsed Japan's occupation of the Shandong Peninsula. In addition, they refused to address China's request for redress of the unequal treaties. The Chinese people were horrified at this betrayal. Their consternation became more profound when it was revealed that the Beijing government had secretly agreed in September 1918 to Japanese operations in the peninsula.

Mao (far right) posed for this photograph with his father (second from left) and brother Zemin (far left) in 1919. His father died of typhoid a year later, and Zemin was murdered in 1943 by a warlord sympathetic to Mao's Nationalist enemies.

Sun Yat-sen with his second wife, Soong Ching-ling. Sun formed the *Guomindang*, or Nationalist party, in 1912. With prodding from the Soviet Union, his major source of aid, Sun allied the Guomindang with the fledgling CCP in 1924.

On May 4, 1919, more than 5,000 students marched in Beijing to protest the Allied decision. In the wake of the Beijing demonstration, anti-Japanese boycotts, strikes, and demonstrations were staged throughout China. Faced with this wave of protest, which became known as the May Fourth Movement, the government in Beijing capitulated, announcing that the Chinese delegation to the peace conference would not accept the Allied decision and would refuse to sign the final peace treaty.

The May Fourth Movement had considerable impact in Hunan. Students went on strike, and dozens of underground newspapers and magazines sprang up. Mao helped organize the United Students Association of Hunan and was editor of their newspaper, the *Hsiang River Review*, for which he also wrote articles explaining the significance of the Allied betrayal at the Paris peace conference.

Mao also wrote a number of pieces in favor of women's rights. When a young Hunanese woman committed suicide rather than marry the groom selected for her by her parents, Mao wrote a series of articles attacking the tradition of arranged marriages as an outdated superstition. These articles attracted the attention of the authorities, and the *Hsiang River Review* was shut down. Mao and other student activists were told by Hunan's governor, Zhang Jingyao, to halt their activities. Mao, however, continued to write, and his reputation as an effective and articulate activist and journalist began to spread. Soon, a leading Changsha newspaper, *Great Welfare Daily*, began buying his articles, and Mao developed a wider readership.

In December 1919 Zhang's troops attacked a crowd burning Japanese goods in a public square. A protest strike erupted immediately, closing down the entire city. Mao wrote a manifesto calling for Zhang's overthrow. Thousands of people signed it, and a rumor that Zhang had ordered Mao's assassination soon began to spread. Conveniently, Mao had already left Changsha to travel to the central government offices in Beijing at the head of a delegation of petitioners who were demanding Zhang's dismissal.

Chiang Kai-shek, who succeeded Sun as head of the Guomindang, at the tomb of the Ming dynasty emperors in Nanjing. By 1928 Chiang had defeated the warlords and established a government, but a trip to the Soviet Union in 1923 had left him with a hatred of communism that made civil war inevitable.

Nationalist cavalry in 1925. The united front of the Guomindang and the CCP ended in April 1927 when Chiang's troops massacred the Communists in Shanghai. The Communists had mistakenly believed that the Nationalists were going to provide them with reinforcements after their successful uprising there.

Mao and his fellow petitioners soon discovered that the Beijing government had little interest in the regional problems of Hunan. While in Beijing, Mao read Marx and Friedrich Engels's *Communist Manifesto* for the first time, and it was probably soon after that Mao committed himself to a socialist revolution as the solution to China's problems.

Mao also used his time in Beijing to renew his friendship with Yang Kaihui. Shortly before Mao's arrival, Professor Yang died of pneumonia. Mao's father died a short time afterward. With the necessity of seeking paternal approval removed, Mao and Yang Kaihui began a trial marriage, a commonplace practice among student supporters of the May Fourth Movement. They were legally married in Changsha a year later.

After four months in Beijing, the delegation closed up its headquarters and returned to Hunan. Yang Kaihui moved back to Changsha with her widowed mother, while Mao decided to visit Shanghai before heading home. Chen Duxiu was trying to persuade his study circle that China needed a communist party. Chen convinced Mao to begin a party in Changsha, where, because of Zhang's brutal rule, many people would almost certainly prove receptive to the idea that radical change could be brought about only by revolution.

When Mao returned to Changsha, he set about looking for a good job to be able to support himself and Yang Kaihui while working for the revolutionary cause. Within a few weeks he found employment as director of a primary school, and he settled in with Yang Kaihui in an elegant, rented house in a pleasant part of the city. The couple's first son, Mao Anying, was born in 1921. With Mao's father's death, he was also responsible for the welfare of his two brothers and his adopted sister. He made certain that all three were enrolled in good schools.

In 1921 the *Comintern* ordered the fusion of all the Marxist study groups in China into a single united party. (Comintern is short for Communist International. It was formed by Lenin in 1921 to direct the international socialist movement.) Chen and Li then organized a conference to carry out that task. In the summer of 1921, Mao and 11 other delegates, representing among them a total of 57 Marxist study groups, met in the French concession of Shanghai for the First Congress of the Chinese Communist party (CCP). Also present was a Comintern agent, Gregory Voitinsky. The gathering was cloaked in secrecy to avoid police harassment.

For the next six years Mao followed the decisions of the CCP, emphasizing the importance of recruiting workers to the revolutionary cause. He helped organize railway workers, seamen, fishermen, construction workers, and rickshaw pullers into unions and discussion clubs. He also conducted an organization drive among the coal miners of Anyuan. At the same time, Mao thought frequently about recruiting peasants to the revolutionary cause. At party meetings he began to encourage his comrades to take more account of the peasants as a prospective revolutionary class. By the early 1920s the Hunan labor movement had grown impressively, but the entire CCP had fewer than 200 members, most of whom were middle-class intellectuals.

When the CCP met for its third congress, in the summer of 1923, Mao had done so much trade union organizing that he was elected to the party's central committee as chief of the organizing bureau.

In China's central, southern and northern provinces, several hundred million peasants will rise like a mighty storm, like a hurricane, a force so swift and violent that no power, however great, will be able to hold it back. They will smash all the trammels that bind them and rush forward along the road to liberation.
—MAO ZEDONG

By the end of 1922, the Comintern had decided that the CCP should accept Sun Yat-sen as the leader of the struggle for national liberation. In January 1924 Sun Yat-sen signed an agreement with the CCP. The CCP would maintain a separate existence, with members in the Guomindang, but they would be permitted no role in the Guomindang leadership.

Mao was upset with this arrangement and took a leave of absence from the party to visit Shaoshan, his favorite retreat since the death of his father. While he was gone, a strike at the Anyuan coal fields was violently suppressed, and the police were looking for him. He immediately moved out of Changsha, leaving Kaihui and their son with her mother.

At the Fourth Congress of the CCP, in January 1925, speaker after speaker voiced suspicions about the Guomindang's interest in the peasantry. (The Guomindang's Peasant Department had established a Peasant Movement Training Institute in July 1924.) Mao had worked so closely with the Guomindang throughout 1924 that some of the CCP members suspected his devotion to the cause. He was accused of "right opportunism" and did not win reelection to the central committee, but he did not seem to care. He went back to Hunan for a vacation with Kaihui and their two small boys and decided to stay there for a while to test out his theories on recruiting peasants to the CCP. The family

This photograph of Mao (standing, third from left) and some of his comrades from the 1927 Hunan Autumn Harvest Uprising was taken in Shaanxi 10 years later. The uprising failed, but in its aftermath Mao formed the nucleus of what would become the Red Army.

farm at Shaoshan became his organizing base. Six months later, when the governor of Hunan ordered his arrest for agitating among the villagers, Mao fled to Guangzhou, where he resumed his work with the Guomindang, editing that organization's main newspaper, *Political Weekly*, and lecturing at the Peasant Movement Training Institute.

By the end of 1924, Sun Yat-sen was on the brink of a unification conference with the pro-Japanese government in Beijing. It seemed as though a democratic election for a national assembly was now a possibility. Mao thought the Guomindang had illusions about sharing power with the warlords, but the CCP leadership, in agreement with Moscow, was preaching a revolution in two stages — first a bourgeois-democratic revolution, and then the socialist revolution. Before the theory could be tested, Sun Yat-sen died of cancer on March 12, 1925.

While Sun Yat-sen had been alive, the fragile collaboration between the Guomindang and the CCP had been maintained, but after his death, control of the Guomindang was quickly grabbed by the party's military wing, headed by Chiang Kai-shek, Sun's top military officer and commandant of the Guomindang's Huangpu Military Academy. Hungry for power and about to marry into one of the wealthiest families in China, Chiang was not about to allow socialist ideas to spoil his plans. A dispute between the Guomindang and the CCP was inevitable.

Until the spring of 1925, the CCP was no more than a thorn in the side of the Guomindang. But in May of that year, the killing of a Chinese worker by a Japanese foreman, in a textile mill in Shanghai, triggered a strike by 500,000 workers. A general strike staged by Chinese workers in the British colony of Hong Kong lasted more than a year, and in Beijing even the rickshaw boys, who depended on foreigners for a livelihood, hung signs from their vehicles that read: No English or Japanese. Chinese Communists played leading roles in the protests. By November 1925, CCP membership had grown from 1,000 to 10,000.

> *His [Chiang's] one passion now became and remained an overriding lust for power. All his politics revolved about the concept of force. He had grown up in a time of treachery and violence. There were few standards of human decency his early warlord contemporaries did not violate; they obeyed no law but power, and Chiang outwitted them at their own game.*
> —THEODORE WHITE and ANNALEE JACOBY
> American historians

Chiang Kai-shek initially showed little concern at these developments. While the Communists were involved in social movements, his Soviet-armed and -trained armies had been busy taking territory. The Guomindang controlled much of southern China and had established a government in Guangzhou. A march to northern China was planned to defeat the warlords and unify the country.

At the Peasant Movement Training Institute and in the pages of *Political Weekly*, Mao urged the peasants to support the northern expedition. Zhou Enlai, a leading CCP member and Chiang's political commissar, supported Mao's position. Zhou, too, believed that the peasantry could help Chiang's forces defeat the warlords and then take charge of the revolution themselves. Mao and Zhou had become close friends, despite the fact that they came from dissimilar backgrounds and had different personalities. Zhou, who came from a middle-class family, had been educated abroad and had joined the CCP while he was in Europe.

During his time at the Peasant Movement Training Institute, Mao predicted that the movement would "rise like a tornado or tempest — a force so extraordinarily swift and violent that no power, however great, will be able to suppress it." At first it seemed that he was right. Literally millions of peasants joined peasant unions and rose up against the landlords as Chiang's armies advanced. It soon became apparent that the right-wing leaders of the Guomindang were making deals with their landlord friends. At CCP meetings, party members angrily proposed pulling out of the Guomindang-CCP "united front." Chiang, for his part, was being urged to expel the Communists from the Guomindang. The Comintern's representative in China, a veteran Bolshevik named Mikhail Borodin, who was acting under orders from Soviet dictator Joseph Stalin, sternly opposed such proposals. Mao himself feared that a split in the Guomindang would only bolster the warlords.

In the summer of 1926, the Guomindang armies entered Changsha. At the time, Hunan was in the grip of a terrible famine, and the hungry peasants, thinking the Guomindang troops would defend their actions, rose up and took rice and pigs from the silos and pens of the wealthy landlords. The CCP leadership feared, with reason, that the peasants' action would upset conservative elements within the Guomindang and would damage the united front. Chiang was outraged by the peasants' initiative, and he removed several Communists from the Guomindang leadership bodies. He did not, however, expel them. He realized that the Communists were the only ones who had any influence over the rampaging Hunanese peasants.

During this period, Mao stayed at home in Shaoshan, writing his *Report on an Investigation of the Peasant Movement in Hunan*. He felt totally vindicated by the revolutionary behavior of the peasants in Hunan and argued that the revolutionary actions of the peasantry could not be subordinated to the political goals of the united front. *Report* created an uproar in the CCP. Chen and the rest of the leadership were startled by Mao's open attack on the party's contention, which reflected both classical Marxist thinking and the policy directives is-

Mikhail Borodin (left) was sent by the Soviet Union to advise the Guomindang and the CCP in 1927. Mao argued that Marxist doctrine had to be considered in light of China's own unique conditions and history.

Qu Qiubai became head of the CCP in August 1927. Mao was denounced by the CCP leadership for the failure of the Autumn Harvest Uprising in Hunan, but he was convinced it was the party that was in error.

sued by the Comintern, that even in China the workers would "take the farmers by the hand and lead them to the revolution."

Mao's *Report* also disturbed Chiang because of its undisguised call for the peasants to seize the land and the power in the countryside. To make matters worse, in March 1927 Zhou and several members of the Guomindang organized another general strike, followed by an armed uprising in Shanghai, where Chiang's future father-in-law, Charles Soong, was head of the Central Bank of China. The uprising was successful, and Zhou proclaimed a citizens' government while he waited for Chiang and Guomindang troops to provide reinforcement against warlord reprisal, as had been agreed upon. Soong, who was dependent on the rich merchants and foreign industrialists who had been hurt by the strike, went to Chiang with a massive bribe and an offer from his friends. If Chiang agreed to march into Shanghai and get rid of the Communists and their supporters, Soong and his powerful friends would see to it that Chiang ruled all China.

Early on the morning of April 12, 1927, Chiang's troops entered Shanghai to mobilize against the Communists, who were based in the working-class districts. The first Communists they encountered — those on guard duty — were taken by surprise. Then, when the main body of the workers' militia responded to the emergency, Chiang's alliance with Soong and Soong's friends in the Shanghai underworld began to pay immediate dividends; gangsters, disguised as workers, murdered the union leaders. As a result, the workers' militia became an army without officers. The ill-equipped workers soon fell back; their rifles and pistols were no match for the Guomindang's machine guns. More than 4,000 workers were massacred in the first round of fighting, and then the Guomindang troops fanned out to hunt down more Communists. Guomindang trucks then loaded up the corpses and dumped them outside Shanghai. In the main square, the heads of well-known Communists and labor leaders were put on public display in bamboo cages. One of the few survivors was Zhou Enlai. Atrocities as terrible as those committed in Shanghai were repeated all over China. In Changsha, Guomindang troops opened fire on labor union and student offices, crying "Long live Chiang!" Thousands of Chinese peasants and workers were murdered that summer.

The Soviet response threw the CCP into utter confusion. The Comintern denounced Chiang as a "traitor to the people and an instrument of imperialism" and at the same time insisted that the united front could not be dissolved. In a matter of weeks the CCP had lost 15,000 members. Most of them had been killed, while the others had resigned in disgust at Moscow's orders. The remaining members of the CCP held their fifth congress in secret. One group of outraged Guomindang members now joined the CCP in protest against the Shanghai betrayal.

At the fifth congress, the weakened and demoralized CCP leadership argued for immediate armed retaliation against the Guomindang. An uprising in Guangzhou was proposed. Mao's contention that resistance would be crushed unless it took place in areas of strong peasant support was rejected by the majority of his colleagues. He angrily denounced the Comintern and Chen for blindly advocating the application of Soviet revolutionary philosophy and methods to Chinese conditions.

With the help of the Soong family and their friends, Chiang had effectively made himself ruler of China. In December 1927 he married Soong Meiling, Charles Soong's youngest daughter. Six months later he captured Beijing, and in October 1928 Chiang's National Government of China was inaugurated in Nanjing.

In the meantime Mao acceded to the CCP directive to organize the Autumn Harvest Uprising in Hunan. The rebellion was a failure. By October 1927 the CCP was in disarray. The party's urban cadres had been routed, and the CCP leadership doubted that a peasant-based revolution could be successful. Mao and a handful of troops retreated to the mountains of Jinggangshan, where he planned his next moves.

4

Democratic Communism

Mao intended to use Jinggangshan as a sanctuary where he and his men could reorganize prior to commencing a campaign of guerrilla warfare. He also planned to set up a model revolutionary regime at Jinggangshan, an ideal democratic community that he hoped would attract the attention and the support of China's masses. He instructed his men to be helpful and courteous to the peasants in the surrounding areas, to assist them in planting and harvesting, and always to return borrowed tools and implements. He declared rape, which at that time most Chinese soldiers considered no more reprehensible than stealing or torture, punishable by death. All decisions were arrived at democratically, and supplies were shared equally. Officers had extra responsibilities but no special privileges.

In 1928 Li Lisan became the head of the CCP but the party's policies remained the same. Mao was relieved of his party duties. Acccording to the CCP he was now merely a military commander, but Mao was no longer overly concerned with CCP directives.

The army must become one with the people so that they see it as their own army. Such an army will be invincible.
—MAO ZEDONG

Mao began his love affair with He Zizhen, his second wife, in mid-1928, while he was regrouping his forces in the mountains of Jinggangshan following the failed Autumn Harvest Uprising. His first wife, Yang Kaihui, remained in Changsha and was killed by the Nationalists in 1930.

Lin Biao was one of the Red Army's ablest generals. He was only 19 when he joined Mao at Jinggangshan but had already commanded a Guomindang platoon and led Communist troops in an uprising at Nanchang.

Shortly after, Mao allied himself with Zhu De Chu Teh, a Communist general who had also suffered setbacks in the Autumn Harvest Uprising. Mao and Zhu were then joined by Lin Biao, who, although only 19, had already proven himself to be a general of considerable talent. The new army created by the fusion of Mao and Zhu's forces fought its first battle a few weeks later, decisively defeating a local warlord.

During this period, Kaihui stayed in Changsha with Mao's two sons. The long separations had caused Mao to drift away from her, and in mid-1928 he fell in love with a local high school girl of 18, He Zizhen. Her father was a small landowner who had joined the CCP in 1927. He Zizhen held a prominent position in the local Communist Youth League and had been assigned to help Mao with his paperwork.

By the spring of 1928 the CCP could no longer afford to mock or ignore Mao's forces. Instead, the party moved to bring them back under party control by officially recognizing them as the fourth Red Army, with Zhu as commander in chief and Mao as political commissar. In early 1929 Peng Dehuai and more than 1,000 men joined Mao in Jinggangshan. Using Jinggangshan as a base, Mao and the Red Army moved outward into Hunan and Jiangxi, implementing land reform as they went. Mao knew that the peasants were used to the armies of the warlords, who were at best undisciplined and at worst little more than murderers, rapists, and thieves. The well-behaved Red Army was unlike anything they had seen before, and won Mao many recruits. By early 1929 Mao commanded more than 100,000 men. Other Communist leaders established themselves along the borders of Hunan, Hubei, Anhui, and Zhejing.

At the same time, Mao sent a report to the CCP headquarters in Changsha, trying to convince his comrades of the value of his methods. "The reasons why the Red Army can sustain itself without collapse in spite of such a poor standard of material life and such incessant fighting is its practice of democracy," he wrote. "The newly captured soldiers in particular feel that our army and the [Nationalist] army are worlds apart. The fact that the same soldier who was not brave in the enemy army yesterday becomes very brave in the Red Army today shows precisely the impact of democracy."

General Zhu De joined Mao at Jinggangshan and helped establish the Communist soviet in Jiangxi province. The collaboration between Mao and Zhu was so close that the peasants often referred to the Red Army as the Zhu-Mao army.

Peng Dehaui deserted from the Guomindang and brought Mao 1,000 reinforcements in 1929, enabling the Red Army to move outward from Jinggangshan into Jiangxi and Hunan provinces.

The CCP leadership ignored Mao's report and, in 1929, ordered Mao to dissolve the Red Army, which would be arranged into small guerrilla units. They instructed Mao to come to Shanghai to help rebuild the party's urban strength, maintaining that peasant uprisings could wait. Mao refused. It is wrong, he said, "to dread the development of the strength of the peasants, to believe that it would harm the revolution if the strength of the peasants were to surpass the leadership of the workers." He remained in Jiangxi, where the Red Army took further territory and recruited more peasants to its cause. He proclaimed the establishment of the Jiangxi "soviet" (the term was first used during the Russian Revolution to refer to workers' councils). The Communist-controlled area within Jiangxi functioned essentially as a separate state.

By early 1930 Mao believed he had enough support to seize power in central China. Li ordered attacks on Changsha, Wuhan, and Nanjing and predicted that the workers would rise up to join the Communists. The anticipated support did not materialize, and the Red Army withdrew in disarray. After the costly failure of the attacks on the cities, the CCP leaders still refused to endorse guerrilla tactics, but they did reinstate Mao to his seat on the politburo. They were in no position to ignore the fact that Mao and his Red Army now had control over 3 million people and 11,000 square miles of territory.

Chiang was also conscious of the growth of the Red Army, and he decided that the time had come to launch "extermination campaigns" against the Communists. Although the Nationalist troops outnumbered the Red Army's by 10 to 1, during 3 concerted campaigns in 1930 and 1931 the Nationalists could not weaken the Red Army's hold on Jiangxi. Lured unawares into Communist-controlled territory, Chiang's men would fan out in small, battalion-size units only to be ambushed and repulsed by the guerrillas. Many demoralized Nationalist troops deserted, and the Red Army's supply of guns, ammunition, and radio sets increased.

One casualty of the Nationalist offensive was Mao's wife, Yang Kaihui, who was captured in Changsha. After being tortured, she was publicly beheaded. Mao's sister was also executed.

In 1931 a new faction took control of the CCP leadership from Li Lisan. Wang Ming and Bo Gu, two young Moscow-trained students who were members of a pro-Moscow grouping within the CCP known as the "28 Bolsheviks," were promoted to top positions in the politburo. Mao was not particularly impressed with the new leaders, who knew a vast amount of Marxist theory but lacked practical experience.

In the fall, Japan, bent on establishing an Asian empire, invaded and conquered Manchuria, China's three northeasternmost provinces, gaining control of 500,000 square miles of Chinese territory. Chiang, more concerned about his war against the Communists, opened negotiations with the Japanese and retreated to Fujian province. Mao and Zhu immediately declared war on Japan, and a large number of Nationalist soldiers, more antiforeign than anticommunist, went over to the Red Army.

In 1931 the Nationalists fought to repel the Japanese invasion of Manchuria, but Chiang believed that the Communists were a greater danger to China than the Japanese and soon resumed his "extermination" campaigns against them.

The Communists were able to win the loyalty of the peasants because their programs promised an end to the harsh lives the peasantry had known under the warlords and Qing emperors. Chiang promised reform, but under the Nationalists taxes were higher than ever.

On November 7, 1931, the First National Soviet Congress of China was held in Ruijin, with 610 delegates in attendance. Mao was declared chairman of the Soviet Republic of China, and the following year the main headquarters of the CCP was moved to the Jiangxi base. While Mao controlled the government and the Red Army, he had little influence in the CCP. Trouble started the moment the leadership arrived. They demanded that all the local peasants — around 500,000 people — be drafted into the Red Army. Mao pointed out that if this were done, there would be no one to grow food, and they would all starve. CCP leaders then pressed again for attacks on the cities. Mao refused.

The 28 Bolsheviks made it patently obvious that they considered Mao a ridiculous, anti-intellectual peasant guerrilla supported by bandits and illiterates. Slowly they stripped away Mao's powers until he had much moral authority but very little say in decision making at Ruijin.

In the winter of 1932–33, Chiang brought 400,000 troops to Jiangxi in an effort to encircle and isolate the Red Army. The CCP central committee insisted that the Red Army mass its forces and defend its territory. The Communists, though they lost considerable amounts of men and territory, managed to repel the invaders.

Over the next two years the situation of the Communists continued to deteriorate. Chiang, aided by two recently arrived German military advisers, Generals Hans von Seecht and Alexander Falkenhausen, started another encirclement campaign in the fall of 1934. By summer the Red Army was surrounded by almost 1 million Nationalist troops and was unable to obtain food or weapons. The military strategy of the 28 Bolsheviks had been completely discredited. Mao was reinstated to his seat on the military council.

A few days later, Mao and Zhou reviewed the situation together. The two agreed that the Communist forces had no choice but to withdraw. Everyone was assigned to units led by Mao, Lin Biao, Zhu, or Zhou Enlai. Final decisions on policy and strategy would be made by Bo Gu and Otto Braun, a German Communist assigned by the Comintern to serve as military adviser. On October 16, 1934, the Red Army, a few thousand civilians, and a few hundred women and children slipped out of the base area through the less well guarded sections of the Nationalist lines. Suicide squads distracted the Nationalist guards during the getaway. He Zizhen, now Mao's wife, accompanied him, but their two infant children were left behind with peasant families in Jiangxi, as were Mao's youngest brother and his wife, He Zizhen's sister. All four of them disappeared after the Nationalists overran the area.

It took two days for Chiang's forces to realize that their prey had gone. The Red Army thus had two days' head start on what would turn out to be a 6,000-mile retreat. Morale was low, the leadership was divided, and no destination had been agreed upon. Few would have predicted that a year later, Mao Zedong would be a hero throughout China and the undisputed leader of the Chinese revolution.

5

March to Glory

It took the Red Army more than a month to get all the way through Chiang's lines. During that time, more than 30 percent of the Communist force was destroyed. Four hundred thousand Nationalist troops followed in hot pursuit, bragging that their enemy would be mowed down before they could cross the first main waterway—the Xiang River.

From the outset, the Communists' attempt to escape seemed doomed to fail, and Mao became increasingly despondent at the tactics of the party leadership, whose military experience was negligible. When the Communists reached the Xiang River, they found most of the crossing points guarded. The Nationalists had ordered the local fishermen to moor their boats on the opposite bank. The Communists knew that if they did not cross, they would be destroyed from the rear. Hastily they put together crude rafts and began ferrying people across while they defended the riverbank against the first Nationalist contingents. Mao wanted to surround the area and use guerrilla tactics against the enemy,

Fight, fail, fight again, fail again, fight again . . . till their victory; that is the logic of the people.
—MAO ZEDONG

The Long March was a 6,000 mile strategic retreat by the Communists to escape encirclement by the Nationalists in Jiangxi. At the Chuishui River in Guizhou province in late January 1935, the Red Army won a crucial encounter with a large Guomindang force.

Mao sought to win the allegiance of the peasants in the areas the Red Army passed through on the Long March. The Communist troops were instructed to treat the peasants with courtesy and pay a fair price for anything they took.

but the party leadership ordered him to conduct a standard frontal attack. Their decision cost thousands of lives. Many of the Communists now began to complain about the party leaders, suggesting that Mao should be in charge of the operation.

In the days that followed, enemy planes practiced new bombing techniques on the Red Army. Mao urged the leaders to revise their tactics and have the Red Army march only at night. This time the leadership listened. Mao also stressed that the army maintain its discipline. There was to be no stealing, no raping, no mistreatment of the local populations. The peasants had to be able to see the difference between the Red Army and the Nationalists.

As the march continued, many peasants left their land and joined the Communists. To educate them, Mao started a March and Study Program, which was taught by those Red Army troops who had had extensive political education.

At a meeting held in Zunyi, in Guizhou province, in early 1935, Mao criticized the politburo, blaming them for the heavy losses that the Red Army had suffered. Once again Mao urged the use of guerrilla tactics to confuse Chiang's forces. Then he made a political proposal, offering a new slogan to explain the Communist withdrawal. Instead of referring to their march as a retreat, they would announce to all of China that the Red Army was on its way north to fight the Japanese invaders, whom the cowardly traitor Chiang refused to confront. Mao argued that his approach would neutralize even the most hostile warlords as well as many antiforeign Nationalist soldiers.

After he finished speaking, Bo Gu offered an angry and defensive response. Zhu De and Zhou Enlai then spoke up to agree with Mao. Mao was named chairman of the politburo and the military council, with the power to make all decisions.

Nationalist soldiers carrying a coffin in Beijing. Although the retreating Red Army was outnumbered and ill equipped, the Nationalists were demoralized by Mao's guerrilla tactics and their inability to lure the Communists into a decisive battle.

General Peng later said that he remembered the Long March as one great battle. With no specific destination in mind, Mao used deception and his precepts of military war to stay ahead of the Nationalists. The Communists marched in one direction, only to turn and move in the opposite direction when the Nationalists were sure they knew where the Communists were going. A small group of Communists would move to the east, and while the Nationalists moved in that direction, the main body of the Communists moved north. They crossed and recrossed rivers, chose the most difficult routes. In the areas they passed through they redistributed land to the peasants. The Communists' egalitarianism, discipline, and patriotism won them many adherents among the peasants.

Mao would later describe how the Red Army had "turned defeat into victory." He told the famed French writer André Malraux — whose masterpiece, the novel *Man's Fate*, portrayed the early days of the Chinese Revolution — that the peasants "soon saw that there was no privileged class among us. They saw that we all ate the same food and wore the same clothes. In the liberated areas, life was less terrible."

By April 1935 the marchers were well ahead of Chiang's pursuers when an advance contingent

An iron smelter in a Communist hand grenade plant. The Nationalists were much better equipped than the Communists, but Mao believed that men, not weapons, won wars, and the support of the peasantry enabled the Communists to survive.

crossed the Yangzi River on the Sichuan-Yunnan border. Ahead was the Dadu River, cutting a torrential path through a deep mountain gorge. The last of the Taiping rebels had been trapped in this very gorge by Qing warlords. Lin Biao rushed ahead with an advance battalion and hid in narrow mountain passes while five scouts went down to the river and seized a ferry at the village of Anshunchang. Spotted by Nationalist aircraft, they crossed to the east bank of the Dadu under a rain of bombs and captured two other ferries. A strong current made the crossings slow, and as the ferries began shuttling the troops across the river, it was clear that Nationalist troops would reach the river before all the Communists had crossed.

Mao sent 200 men of the Red Army's elite Fourth Shock Regiment 100 miles north to seize the iron suspension bridge at Luding, the only bridge across the Dadu. For two days and nights the Red Army scouts marched along the narrow path, on the west bank of the Dadu. At several points they fought skirmishes with Nationalist troops, and on the second night they could see the torches of the Nationalist troops across the river. Late that second night they jogged along the footpath so as to reach the bridge by morning. Failure to secure the bridge meant the likely destruction of the Red Army and the probable end of the Chinese Revolution. Fewer than half of them reached Luding, only to be faced with a terrible sight. Half of the bridge's planks had been removed, leaving only 13 iron chains. On the opposite cliff Nationalist troops armed with machine guns had dug in. Twenty-two Red soldiers volunteered to make the crossing. With grenades pinned to their shirts and rifles strapped to their backs, they crawled hand over hand along the great iron chains, 200 feet above the roaring waters and jagged rocks. Machine-gun fire ricocheted off the chains and cliffs. Behind them came the other men of the Fourth Shock Regiment, laying down planks over the chains. The Nationalist troops set the planks on their side on fire. Still the Reds came on. The Nationalist garrison fled.

Zhou Enlai in the mountains of Shaanxi at the conclusion of the Long March. Zhou's support for Mao at the CCP meeting held in Zunyi in early 1935 had been crucial in making Mao the party's political and military leader.

Following the Red Army's crossing of the Dadu River, the Nationalists virtually abandoned their pursuit of the Communists. They thought it certain that no more than a handful of the Communists could survive the next part of the trek. Indeed, the journey through Jiajinshan (the Great Snowy Mountains) almost destroyed the Red Army. Most of the soldiers were from warm southern China and had little experience with snow or freezing temperatures. The highest peak, Jiajin Mountain, is more than 14,000 feet. Hundreds froze to death or collapsed and died from lack of oxygen. Others simply slid off the icy trails and were killed. Lin Biao collapsed twice at Jiajin's summit and had to be carried down. Mao had to be assisted by his bodyguards. Zhou Enlai became seriously ill and later nearly died.

At Luding Bridge, built in 1701, 22 Red Army soldiers crossed hand-over-hand, hanging from the bridge's chains. Despite Nationalist gunfire, they established a bridgehead on the opposite side that enabled Mao to cross 13,000 of his troops across the Dadu River.

The rest of the journey proved equally difficult. The grasslands of western China were inhabited by Tibetan tribesmen possessed with a long-standing hatred of all Chinese. The Tibetans fled their villages and hid their food as the Red Army advanced. Red Army stragglers were ambushed. The grasslands are essentially marsh and bog. Men were swallowed up and drowned. Hundreds starved to death. When the food was gone, the few remaining horses were killed. Finally the soldiers were reduced to eating boiled grass and bark.

Shortly after passing through the grasslands, the Red Army again entered territory inhabited by Chinese. It was September 1935, and nearly 6,000 miles from their starting point, they felt they were home. To this point Mao had led his forces with no specific destination in mind, but in past days he had learned of the existence of a soviet in Shaanxi. On October 15, 1935, less than 10,000 ragged survivors of the Long March were met by 5 men on horseback, representatives of the Provincial Soviet of Northern Shaanxi. Their commander, Liu Zhidan, an old friend of Mao's, had sent them to welcome the Red Army.

The Liupan Mountains were the last obstacle faced by the Communists on the Long March. On the other side lay Shaanxi province, where the Communists were able to regroup and prepare to carry on the fight.

China, excluding Manchuria and portions of the westernmost areas. The dark line represents the path of the Long March, which only 10 percent of the Red Army survived.

Hundreds of Red Army soldiers died on the trek over Jiajin Mountain, the highest peak in the Great Snowy Mountains of western China. Local superstition had it that only angels could fly over Jiajin, and many of Mao's men remembered the Snowy Mountains as the most difficult portion of the Long March.

It was one of the most remarkable military feats in history. The Long March had covered 6,000 miles, crossed desert, swamp, and mountains, and forded 24 rivers. From it was born the legend of the invincible Red Army. Toughened by battle and hardship, the survivors were unlikely to be fazed by the challenges still before them. Mao wrote one of his many poems about the heroism of the men and women of the Long March:

> The Red Army fears not the rigors of a forced march;
> To them a thousand mountains, ten thousand rivers, are but a gentle walk.
> The Five Ridges ripple by like little waves,
> And the mountain peaks of Wumeng are but mounds.
> Warm are the cloud-topped cliffs above the River of Golden Sand,
> Soft are the iron chains that span the Dadu River.
> Soldiers delight in the ageless snows of Minshan,
> And they smile proudly as the Army crosses.

6

Out of the Ashes

The Long March, Mao said, was both a victory and a defeat. On the one hand, he wrote, "it announced to some 200 million people in 11 provinces that the road of the Red Army is their only road to liberation." On the other hand, he declared, "except for the Shanxi-Gansu border areas, all revolutionary bases were lost, the Red Army reduced from 300,000 to a few tens of thousands."

Mao started rebuilding the Red Army at once. Shaanxi, however, was far from an ideal setting for such an undertaking: two million poverty-stricken people lived in caves carved into hillsides; the land in Shaanxi was not particularly fertile; and parts of the province were frequently subjected to the ravages of desert dust storms and floods of the Yellow River. Still, Mao and the other survivors managed to settle fairly comfortably in Shaanxi. Like everyone else, Mao and He lived in a cave. He had few possessions, and the walls were covered with maps.

Of all the influences that shaped Mao's thinking, the most important were those that stemmed from his personal experiences during the decades before the Communist movement conquered China. And perhaps the most profound of these experiences were the years spent in Yanan.
—STANLEY KARNOW
American writer

Communist troops mobilize in Shaanxi, where Mao established his capital at Yanan. After the Long March Mao turned to fighting the Japanese. As Chiang seemed more eager to rid China of the Communists, Mao's strategy won the Communists the support of patriotic Chinese eager to see their country free of foreign invaders.

Mao worked 14 hours a day, planning future strategy. In December 1935 he called a CCP politburo conference and made a startling proposal. The Chinese Communists, he said, should press Chiang for another united front to smash Japan. The 28 Bolsheviks, who still enjoyed considerable influence within the party, opposed the proposal fiercely. Mao then told the assembled delegates that he loved his country more than he hated Chiang. "We cannot even discuss communism if we are robbed of a country in which to practice it," he reminded them. He won a majority of the delegates, but many believed that his prestige, not his logic, secured his victory.

Mao's decision quickly proved to have been inspired. The Chinese people hated the Japanese and greatly resented their presence in Manchuria, but Chiang resisted Mao's entreaties for a united front. In late 1936 a Manchurian warlord, Zhang Xueliang, captured Chiang at the Shaanxi city of Xian. He offered Mao the opportunity of taking part in a "people's trial" of Chiang, but, possibly under the influence of directions from the Soviet Union, Mao arranged for Chiang's release in exchange for assurances that a truce between the Nationalists and the Communists would be arranged and that Chiang would commit himself to fighting Japan. (At the time, the Soviet Union had committed itself to a united front policy — that is, cooperation between communist movements and noncommunist govern-

Japanese soldiers, wearing headbands of the Japanese flag, were vilified for the brutality of their occupation of China. In December 1937, they executed more than 200,000 civilians in the city of Nanjing.

ments to resist fascism, as practiced by Adolf Hitler in Germany, Francisco Franco in Spain, and Japan's military dictatorship.)

The Red Army moved north to Yanan, a three-day journey on mountain trails, where the steep mountains and deep gorges provided a natural barrier against invasion. Yanan was also a better strategic location for the fight against Japan. Mao made Yanan his base for the next 10 years, from 1937 to 1947. It was there that he worked at perfecting his ongoing experiments in socialist living, prescribing the distinctive mode of existence that became known as the "Yanan Way." In a city of cave dwellings carved in the cliffs, Mao and He fixed up a three-room whitewashed cave where they lived with their new daughter. They lived very simply. Mao still wore his cotton uniform, and children were free to run in and out of their quarters. He followed his own prescription for achieving equality among intellectuals, workers, and peasants: physical labor. Mao worked in the fields to grow his own food and tobacco.

At Yanan, the Communist headquarters until 1947, Mao directed the war against the Japanese and established an economically self-sufficient community designed to serve as a model of what China would be like under the Communists.

Mao at Yanan in 1936. Writer Agnes Smedley, who visited Yanan, noted in Mao a quality of "spiritual isolation." She "had the impression he would wait and watch for years, but eventually have his way."

He Zizhen, though, led a very subdued existence. She had changed from the lively, spirited girl he had taken on the Long March; now she was a sickly and depressed woman. She had been badly wounded during a bombing raid on the Long March; the loss of her children and the entire ordeal had been too much for her. Soon Mao's attention turned to Jiang Qing, a film actress and dabbler in revolutionary politics, who arrived in Yanan in 1937. Although the party objected to Mao's plan to divorce He — who was a valuable comrade whose loyalty had been proven on the Long March — Mao brushed aside their objections. He arranged for He to go to the Soviet Union to receive medical treatment and then married Jiang Qing.

During this period, Mao turned increasingly to writing — this time attacking the tenets of abstract Marxism in favor of a Marxism derived from the conditions and circumstances peculiar to China. He drew up a program for the liberated base area. For the peasants, a new life began. Taxes were abolished, and land could be rented cheaply. Cooperative work was encouraged, and many schools were established. Word of the new Communist capital spread throughout China, and many visitors came, some of whom stayed on. The contrast between life at Yanan and life in the areas held by the Nationalists startled many people. In the Nationalist areas, land reform was nonexistent, poverty and disease rampant, and taxes repressively high. Eighty percent of the revenue collected by Chiang's government went toward military expenditures.

Mao directed the fight against the Japanese employing the same tactics he had used against Chiang, using guerrilla warfare behind the Japanese lines to wear down the invader. Chiang sent bombers to raid Yanan despite his earlier promises of unity. Chiang's reluctance to confront the Japanese and his continued aggression against the Communists, combined with Mao's successes against the Japanese, attracted patriotic and Nationalist Chinese to the Communists. It seemed only the Communists cared enough about China to combat the invader.

In July 1937 Japan launched a full-scale invasion of China. Retreating quickly, Chiang's armies were driven from the cities. By August the Japanese had taken Beijing, and by the summer of 1938 the Japanese armies had taken all of the coastal cities of China. Chiang fell back, leaving Mao's troops, the Eighth Route Army, to carry on the fight behind enemy lines. In full retreat before the Japanese, he abandoned Nanjing and fled to Chongqing. The Japanese slaughtered thousands of civilians in Nanjing. To slow down the Japanese advance, Chiang ordered the dikes blown up behind him. Tens of thousands drowned in dozens of cities and villages. Slow death from starvation took more lives. In the occupied cities, Chinese were used as slave laborers. Those who might previously have been indifferent to Chiang now hated him. The Eighth Route Army, operating in small groups, grew from a force of 40,000 to 400,000 by the spring of 1940. They were no longer called the Red Army, but all of China knew they were Mao's men. Fifty million people lived within Mao's base areas of northern China, and 200,000 of them had joined the CCP.

Chinese soldiers carry unexploded and defused Japanese bombs. Mao advocated a united front with the Nationalists to combat the Japanese, and Chiang agreed, but true cooperation between the two forces was nonexistent.

Chiang's propaganda portrayed the Communists as little more than bandits, but Western journalists who visited Yanan and its environs found a self-sufficient enclave defended by a dedicated, disciplined military and political organization. Shown (from left) are Mao, journalist Earl Leaf, Zhu De, and an unidentified woman.

Chiang Kai-shek felt threatened by the growth of Communist-held territories behind the Japanese lines, and even more threatened by Mao's elevation to the status of a hero by so many of the Chinese people. Chiang engaged in a brutal war of attrition against the Eighth Route Army, successfully blockading the areas it occupied. He received arms, ammunition, and other supplies from the Soviet Union and the United States. It was assumed that the Eighth Route Army would receive a share of this equipment, but after 1939 nothing arrived. Mao's efforts to make the Communist-held areas self-sufficient paid off when aid ground to a halt. Arms and ammunition were no problem: Successful raids against the Japanese assured plenty of those.

It seemed only the Communists were willing to fight the Japanese. The Nationalists refused to mount an attack. In the fall of 1940 the Communists' Hundred Regiments Offensive decisively defeated the Japanese. The Japanese soon recognized that Mao's forces were their greater enemy and directed their efforts at the northern provinces held by the Communists. The Japanese burned villages and destroyed crops and killed one-quarter of the Eighth Route Army's troops and millions of civilians, but their attentions confirmed to many Chinese that only Mao was interested in defending

China. In the eyes of the Chinese people, it was the Communists who were identified with anti-imperialism. Between 1937 and 1945 (when Japan surrendered at the end of World War II), the Communist army grew from 50,000 to 500,000, and the Communists expanded their control to over 100 million Chinese—one-fifth of the population.

Except for Soviet aid to Chiang's Nationalists and a boycott of Japanese goods by private citizens in the United States, the world was not paying much attention to events in China in 1941. The armies of German fascist dictator Adolf Hitler had swept through western Europe in 1940 and poured east into the Soviet Union in 1941, events which launched World War II.

The United States was still trying to avoid involvement in a European war when Japanese planes suddenly bombed Pearl Harbor, a U.S. naval base in Hawaii, on December 7, 1941. The United States declared war on the Axis powers — Germany, Italy, and Japan — and joined the Allies — Great Britain, the Soviet Union, and France.

At Yanan in 1937 Mao met film actress Jiang Qing (pictured), who became his third wife. He Zizhen, his second wife, had been very badly wounded on the Long March and had never recovered emotionally from the ordeal. In 1938 Mao divorced He, and she was quietly dispatched to Moscow for medical treatment.

A Chongqing woman and her two children in the wreckage of their home following a Japanese air raid. More than 2 million Chinese died in the war with Japan. The Communists' image as the patriotic defenders of the homeland enabled them to greatly expand their influence in the country.

China now became an important strategic area, especially for Japan, which considered China a potential base for control of the whole Pacific. Likewise, the United States had an interest in a strong Chinese resistance, which for a time would tie up valuable Japanese troops and resources. From the Chinese point of view, U.S. aid would be invaluable to fight the Japanese. Eager for U.S. weapons and dollars, Chiang agreed to renew the united front. The United States named him supreme commander of the Chinese element of the China-Burma-India (CBI) theater of war.

At first, U.S. journalists and politicans paid no attention to Mao. They came to China to consult with Chiang, who received most of the U.S. aid. But journalist Theodore White's description of Nationalist behavior during a famine in Hunan shocked the public. "The peasants . . . were dying. And as they died, the government continued to wring from them the last possible ounce of taxes . . . their loyalty had been hollowed to nothingness by the extortion of their government."

The United States's China policy took many directions over the next few years. In early 1942 U.S. general Joseph W. Stilwell was appointed Chiang's chief of staff in Chongqing. Stilwell had spent over a dozen years in China and spoke the language. He was ordered to encourage unified operations against the Japanese by Chiang's and Mao's forces. The United States feared that Chiang, to save his own skin, would make peace with Japan. While Mao agreed to join a coalition government, Chiang refused. Stilwell then went to his superior, the U.S. Army chief of staff, General George C. Marshall. He told Marshall that Chiang was "head of a one-party government supported by a Gestapo and a party secret service. . . . What we should do is shoot the generalissimo." Chiang was, in fact, avoiding battle to finish the war with a large stock of arms and ammunition for the task he considered most important — destroying Mao's forces. He was quite content to let the U.S. Air Force in China — the famed "Flying Tigers" under Cláire Chennault — do the bulk of his fighting for him.

Stilwell's final summation was that Chiang "can't see that the mass of Chinese people welcome the Reds as being the only visible hope of relief from crushing taxation and the abuses of the army. . . . The cure for China's trouble is the elimination of Chiang." In April 1944 Japan launched its last and biggest military offensive in southern and central China, routing Chiang's troops and gaining over 100,000 square miles of territory. Over 700,000 Nationalist troops were lost.

In July 1944 a U.S. Army observer mission came to Yanan. Mao spent a great deal of time talking with the Americans. At age 51, Mao still had a boyish look about him. Members of the mission described him as friendly toward the United States. He engaged them in lively discussions about democracy and the American Revolution. Mao sought to convince the Americans that the reforms he had in mind for China were moderate and just, and the Americans were impressed by the democratic functioning of Mao's headquarters and the entire base area.

> *The Japanese are a disease of the skin; the Communists are a disease of the heart.*
> —CHIANG KAI-SHEK

U.S. ambassador Patrick Hurley (right) accompanied Mao (left) on his August 1945 trip from Yanan to Chongqing. There Mao met with Chiang Kai-shek to discuss the possible establishment of a coalition government and an end to civil war between the Communists and the Nationalists.

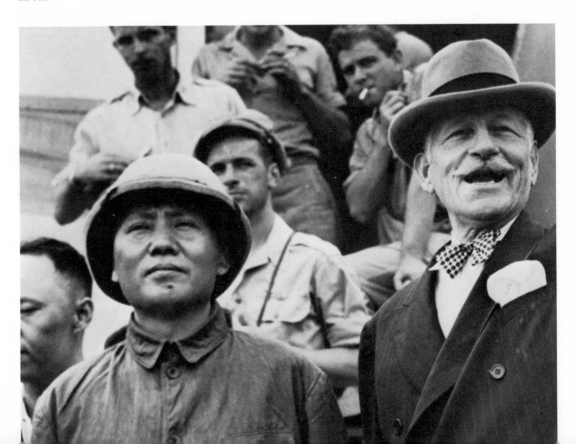

Chiang Kai-shek received enormous amounts of aid from the United States for the war against Japan. The outbreak of World War II in Asia in December 1941 made Chinese resistance to the Japanese crucial to the U.S. war effort.

John P. Davies, a political adviser to Stilwell, and John Service, a U.S. State Department representative, became convinced that their government should abandon its support for Chiang and support Mao instead. "The Communists are in China to stay," Davies reported. Chiang was furious at the findings of the U.S. mission and subsequently demanded that Stilwell be removed from his post in China. Roosevelt gave in, and Stilwell was sent home. Further negotiations to arrange a true united front, with a coalition army, were rebuffed by Chiang.

By the end of 1944, Japan was on the run. U.S. forces had fought their way across the Pacific islands and were being readied for an invasion of Japan. Japan was close to surrender. American supplies were flowing to Chiang, clearly meant for his forthcoming war against Mao. On August 6, 1945, the United States dropped an atomic bomb on the Japanese city of Hiroshima; on August 9, Nagasaki suffered atomic annihilation. Stalin, convinced that the Americans would make Chiang the next ruler of China, belatedly declared war on Japan, sent troops into Manchuria, and signed a treaty with the Nationalists. Just days after the Japanese surrender, Mao received a cabled invitation from Chiang to come to Chongqing for peace talks. U.S. ambassador Patrick Hurley flew to Yanan to urge Mao to accept the invitation. The Soviet government also advised him to accept.

On August 26, Mao flew to Chongqing. With Zhou Enlai by his side, Mao saw city lights for the first time in 13 years. For more than a month he and Chiang negotiated, but they reached no substantive agreement. The Communists were unwilling to accept Guomindang domination of the government and proposed a coalition government; the Nationalists were determined not to share power. Mao was aware that while Chiang was negotiating, he was simultaneously directing Nationalist operations against the Communists. An assassination attempt against Mao heightened his mistrust.

Meanwhile, 120,000 Red Army men under Lin

Biao marched swiftly through Manchuria, confiscating huge stores of surrendered weapons. Men were left behind in each village to educate people and win recruits to the Red Army. Fighting between Nationalist and Red Army formations broke out. A cease-fire was arranged in January 1946, but it was quickly broken when Chiang ordered his secret police to Shenyang and Beijing to arrest Communist members of the cease-fire teams. The Chinese civil war was in full swing. The Nationalists possessed clear-cut military advantages. Their troops outnumbered the Communist forces by four to one and enjoyed a great superiority in weaponry. The Nationalists had an air force while the Communists did not.

The U.S. Congress voted aid to the Nationalists. U.S. advisers trained and equipped 150,000 Nationalist troops, and American planes and ships transported them north. Few Americans knew that almost 100,000 U.S. Marines were also in China, stationed in Beijing, Tianjin, and several other cities. Their official assignment was to protect the coal mines and lines of communication on behalf of Chiang Kai-shek. By mid-October, Chiang had reoccupied most of the cities of the north.

Chinese Communist troops in 1943. The war with Japan was in some ways a boon to Mao, as it established him in the minds of many Chinese as a patriotic, nationalist leader and won the Communists many millions of new supporters.

In March, repeated Nationalist bombings forced the Communists to abandon Yanan. Many of the officers and soldiers wanted to make a last stand, but Mao refused. "It is after all only caves," said Mao. "Empty cities don't matter. The aim is to destroy the enemy's army." Chiang flew to Yanan and bragged to the press that in three months the People's Liberation Army (PLA), as Mao's forces were now known, would be finished.

But the seeds of Chiang's defeat had long been germinating in China. It was no secret that Chiang and the Soong family had profited enormously from their control of the economy. In Manchuria frenzied looting by Nationalist troops disaffected the local population. Chiang's troops were constantly harassed and sabotaged by the peasants. Chiang had the territory, but the PLA was protected everywhere by the peasants. Chiang's troops were savaged from all sides. In the cities a new student movement poured into the streets chanting "Food, Peace, Freedom." Chiang's government repressed the students. A U.S. military observer noted that the Chinese were turning to the Communists because "nothing could be worse than the Guomindang." Prominent intellectuals protested. Mao called the dissent a "second front to the first, armed struggle."

With World War II concluded, Mao and Chiang met at Chongqing in August 1945 and drank to the possibility of a united government for China. Their negotiations were unsuccessful, however, and civil war soon resumed.

By the summer of 1948 Chiang's soldiers were deserting en masse. Bolstered by peasant recruits, the Communist forces grew from 500,000 to 2 million. In the Nationalist areas, Chiang outlawed all opposition, driving more people into the Communist camp. Mao's troops began what became a giant victory march on northern China, with the Nationalists fleeing before them. As 1948 ended, the PLA reached the western hills overlooking Beijing. A Nationalist general negotiated a surrender with Mao's warriors. Crowds stood on the side of the roads as PLA soldiers poured into the city, some of them riding in captured American tanks and jeeps. A peasant army had taken the capital of the world's most populous country. As the PLA soldiers gaped at the lights and buildings of the city, a voice over a loudspeaker congratulated the people of Beijing on their "liberation." Too late, Chiang sent offers from Nanjing to share governmental power with the Communists. Stalin urged Mao to seek an agreement with Chiang. Instead, Mao demanded the unconditional surrender of Chiang's armies. Chiang refused.

Mao continued to direct battles all over the country. He did not arrive in Beijing until almost three months after it had been taken. Then he entered the city that he had known so well as a young man and went straight to the Forbidden City, the home of the Chinese emperors, taking with him Jiang Qing and their daughter. On October 1, 1949, he rode in a huge procession down the main street of Beijing. Ahead of his automobile, a captured U.S.-made tank guarded him. It had been sent to China to help Chiang Kai-shek defeat him. Mao stood on the Gate of Heavenly Peace under a poster of Sun Yat-sen and said, "The Chinese people have stood up . . . nobody will insult them again."

As Mao proclaimed the birth of the People's Republic of China, the last vestiges of Nationalist resistance were crumbling. Chiang and an entourage of Nationalist government officials were ferried over to the island of Taiwan by U.S. ships. He stepped off the Chinese mainland for the last time on December 8, 1949.

Mao with troops in 1947. (Jiang Qing is behind him, in wide-brimmed hat.) Despite being outgunned and outmanned, the Communists won the civil war and came to power in 1949 because the continued suffering of the peasantry under Nationalist rule cost Chiang his chance of commanding the loyalty of the majority of the Chinese people.

7

Choosing Sides

Ensconced at the Imperial Palace, Mao sought to reassemble his children, who were spread all over the globe. Jiang Qing was flying back and forth to Moscow for medical treatment. The civil war had taken a toll on her health. Mao's former wife, He Zizhen, returned from the Soviet Union with their daughter Li Min but soon had to enter a mental institution in Shanghai. Jiang Qing raised Li Min along with her own daughter by Mao, Li Na. Anying and Anqing, Mao's sons by his first wife, Yang Kaihui, had also returned to China from the Soviet Union. Anying worked as a translator of Russian, and Anqing seemed to do very little. He finally returned to the Soviet Union in 1950 for psychiatric treatment.

Mao, at 56, began to show signs of a belief in his own omnipotence. He had done what everyone had said could not be done. Marx, Lenin, Stalin, the entire CCP leadership — none of them had believed in the possibility of a peasant revolution. He was the undisputed hero of the Chinese people. Now he could direct a miraculous reconstruction of China's

Classes struggle, some classes triumph, others are eliminated. Such is history, such is the history of civilization for thousands of years.
—MAO ZEDONG

With the proclamation of the establishment of the People's Republic of China in October 1949, Mao set himself to reconstructing the country, which had been devastated by more than 30 years of nearly continuous warfare, and remolding it into a communist state.

Mao with Anying, one of his two sons by his first wife, Yang Kaihui. After Yang's execution by the Nationalists in 1930, Anying and his brother, Anqing, had lived with some of Mao's relatives in Shanghai and had then been sent to school in the Soviet Union. Anying was killed in a U.S. bombing raid during the Korean War.

government and economy as capably as he had forged the revolution. He first named his trusted comrade Zhou Enlai premier and foreign minister. Mao was given the title of first chairman. Instead of following the Soviet model, he outlined his own policies in an article titled "On the People's Democratic Dictatorship."

To get support from all sides, Mao had discovered it was wise to give leadership to people with many different points of view. In Yanan, noncommunists had participated in the governing bodies. The first government of the People's Republic was a coalition of peasants', workers', and small-businessmen's delegates. Fourteen political parties were represented. Only landlords and upper-class businessmen who had supported Chiang had no voice in government. In this "people's democratic dictatorship" there were elections to a national congress and freedom of speech, assembly, and association.

With an empty treasury, though, financial aid from the outside world was mandatory. There was no point in trying to mend fences with the richest nation on earth, the United States, which had entered into its cold war with the Soviet Union. Anticommunism had become a basic tenet of U.S. foreign policy, and the United States was about to enter a period of anticommunist hysteria, marked by fear of internal communist subversion. Though the United States would rebuild Japan, feed Chiang's forces on Taiwan, and reconstruct Europe, there would be no aid for China. As a result, Mao had little choice but to go to Stalin for aid.

Mao traveled to Moscow in December 1949 and spent two months there. It was his first trip beyond China's borders. The lack of a warm reception startled Mao. Stalin considered Mao an unlettered peasant, unschooled in the fine points of Marxist theory. Mao did not trust Stalin and remembered that it was Stalin who had always urged cooperation with the Guomindang. Stalin now sought territorial and economic concessions in exchange for aid. Nevertheless, Mao persisted and came back with a $300 million low-interest loan and the promise of Soviet technicians and technology in exchange for Soviet control of parts of Manchuria and that joint Soviet-Chinese stock companies would own mineral rights in the western desert areas.

Back in China, corrupt public officials were fired. The Red Army was demobilized, and the former soldiers were sent to work on farms and in old and new factories. Schools, clinics, and housing projects sprang up everywhere. Inflation was kept to a minimum by price controls. The property and wealth formerly controlled by the Guomindang leaders were seized. Private enterprise was taken over by the state. In the countryside "Revolutionary People's Courts" tried landlords and officials who had oppressed the peasants in the past. Landlords had their land confiscated and often were sentenced to death. Several million people were killed during land reform, and the landowning class was largely eliminated. Everywhere, mass democratic meetings were held. To Mao it looked as though the revolutionary spirit of his "Yanan Way" was sweeping China.

World events interrupted Mao's plans. Korea, China's northeastern neighbor, had been divided into two countries after World War II: North Korea under a communist dictator friendly to the Soviet Union, South Korea under a pro-Western dictator

A U.S. Marine (right) guards captured North Korean soldiers. The Korean War broke out in June 1950, when North Korea invaded South Korea. U.S. troops were sent to fight the North Koreans as part of a United Nations peacekeeping mission.

allied to the United States. At the 38th parallel, which separated the two countries, there had been frequent skirmishes between the opposing armies. On June 25, 1950, North Korean forces crossed the parallel. A United Nations army, led by U.S. general Douglas MacArthur, was sent to "keep the peace" in Korea.

North Korean troops gained the early advantage, but MacArthur soon pushed them back and then crossed the 38th parallel into North Korea. As the fighting approached the China-Korea border, Mao sent 250,000 troops to assist the North Koreans. The war ended in a stalemate in 1953, with Korea still divided, approximately along the 38th parallel. The Chinese suffered nearly 1 million casualties, among them Mao's son Anying. Equally important, money and resources that were badly needed to reform China were instead deployed to the war effort.

In 1952 the first Five-Year Plan to modernize China was introduced. Modeled after similar plans of the Soviet Union, it did well. Its emphasis was on developing heavy industry. Iron, steel, coal, and cement production doubled and quadrupled. Dams, bridges, and railways were built. Health conditions improved, and life expectancy soared. In the countryside, land reform had a profound impact. Rent and taxes were abolished, and cooperative movements forged ahead. A "settling of accounts movement" took the possessions of the landlords and distributed them to the poor. Women were allowed to own land and property. In the eyes of the masses, Mao was a magician. His *Selected Works* was serialized in the newspapers, and his words were quoted as gospel all over the country.

In the Soviet Union, Nikita Khrushchev had emerged as the nation's leader following the death of Stalin. Fearful of nuclear warfare, Khrushchev wanted to start a new policy of "peaceful coexistence" with the West. Mao disagreed totally with this policy. Nuclear weapons did not frighten him. Wars would be won with people, not bombs, he said. He called the United States a "paper tiger."

Chinese troops entered the Korean War when predominantly U.S. forces under the command of General Douglas MacArthur approached China's border with Korea. The Chinese involvement was costly in terms of manpower and resources that would have been better employed in reforming and rebuilding China.

Zhou Enlai (at left) and Mongolian delegates celebrate the first anniversary of the People's Republic. Mao's most trusted lieutenant, Zhou became premier and foreign minister.

As each year passed, Mao felt increasingly dissatisfied. No matter how much progress there was, things moved too slowly for him. In 1955 he decided to push the land reform process faster. Liu Shaoqi and other CCP leaders told him he was moving too fast. The peasants, they said, were not ready for such a rapid change. This was the first time Liu had questioned Mao's decisions.

At the 20th Congress of the Communist party of the Soviet Union (CPSU) in Moscow in 1956, Khrushchev made some startling admissions. Stalin, he said, had led a reign of terror against the Soviet people. Millions of Soviet citizens had been executed or interned in labor camps for alleged counterrevolutionary activity. Now there would be a liberalization policy.

During this period the question of free speech began to trouble Mao. Although free speech had been promised, millions of Chinese had been investigated for counterrevolutionary crimes. Although Mao admitted that over 700,000 had been executed, other sources gave a much higher figure. Mao went to Wuhan and Changsha to rest. He disappeared from Beijing for several weeks to figure out his next steps. Then, in February 1957, he made his own startling speech, "On the Correct Handling of Contradictions Among People." He called for debate in every area of life. "In every field let one hundred flowers blossom, and let one hundred schools of thought contend," he announced.

The texts of Voice of America broadcasts and Chiang's speeches were printed in China's newspapers. Liberal intellectuals took Mao's turnabout at face value and made speeches and wrote articles denouncing one-party rule. In Wuhan, students marched through the streets carrying placards that read: "Welcome to the Nationalists! Welcome to Chiang Kai-shek!" This was too much for Mao. He called a halt to the free-speech movement.

The "Hundred Flowers Campaign," as it was later called, was the first of a series of impetuous decisions that would characterize Mao's later years. Instead of mellowing with age, Mao seemed to become increasingly restless, ever more anxious to complete the many tasks still before him.

Accompanying the Hundred Flowers Campaign was the first publication of Mao's poems. Composed over the years of the Revolution, they commemorate such events as the Long March and Jinggangshan. Many celebrated the beauties of nature. Most were written in classical Chinese form and contained allusions to Chinese history and literature. One of Mao's biographers, Jerome Chen, believes that his poems are of sufficient quality to ensure Mao a place in contemporary Chinese literature regardless of his political achievements.

In October 1957 Soviet scientists launched the first man-made satellite, *Sputnik I*, into space. The Soviet Union had signed a new trade pact with China and agreed to help China develop an atomic bomb. "The east wind prevails over the west wind," Mao crowed. The following month, Mao attended a summit of world communist leaders in Moscow. In private conversations, Mao expressed his opinion that U.S.-Soviet disarmament talks were futile. The word must, however, have gotten out to Khrushchev, who had been alarmed by several reckless statements of Mao's regarding the use of nuclear weapons. During the months that followed, instead of scientists to help build a Chinese atomic bomb, only a trickle of outdated information was sent.

Mao with Soviet leader Nikita Khrushchev in the late 1950s. Mao was wary of the Soviets, insisting that in China communism must develop in accordance with Chinese conditions and history and not follow Soviet models. He also questioned the Soviet commitment to worldwide revolution.

News of the cooling of Chinese-Soviet relations reached the United States. Anticommunists in that country made increasingly hostile speeches about Communist China, accusing Mao of being a threat to world peace. Mao answered coldly. The United States, he said, had planes and troops in bases all over the world. China had no armed forces based outside her own borders. The United States spent more than half of a huge budget on the military, China only eight percent of a tiny one.

Behind the scenes, CCP politburo members were attacking Mao's criticisms of Khrushchev's policies. Many of them had also opposed the Hundred Flowers Campaign. The time was not ripe to move against Mao — still the hero of China. But they had noticed a trembling in his hands at the Eighth Congress of the CCP. Mao was getting old; they would bide their time. They did not know it then, but Mao was devising another scheme, one that would shake the Revolution to its very foundations.

8

The Great Leap Forward

By the late 1950s Mao was impatient with the rate of China's economic development. Too much attention had been given to industrialization at the expense of the peasantry, he said. Industrialization should be small-scale, centered in the countryside, Mao decided. Despite objections from several CCP leaders, in 1958 Mao launched a mass movement to carry out his plan, dubbed the "Great Leap Forward." Communes as large as 20,000 people were created, where peasants would not only grow food for themselves but also try to manufacture what they needed — shoes, clothing, pots and pans. Every commune would have its own health clinics, communal laundries, grain mills, power stations, and even backyard steel furnaces. Through sheer will, revolutionary fervor, and massive work battalions, Mao wanted China to accomplish in months what took other countries years.

The true way that governs the world is that of radical change.
—MAO ZEDONG

Mao stressed that people were more important than guns in making a revolution or winning a war. The Great Leap Forward was Mao's attempt to join the revolutionary enthusiasm that had swept the Communists to power with the manpower of the world's most populous nation in order to transform China's economy.

Mao inspects a double-edged plow in 1956. Impatient with China's economic progress, Mao launched the Great Leap Forward in 1958 by reorganizing the peasantry into massive people's communes, intended to be completely self-sufficient. However, poor planning resulted in widespread shortages and near famine.

Five hundred million peasants were suddenly swept into 24,000 communes. The last vestiges of capitalism, such as extra pay or time off, were eliminated. People worked 12 hours a day without additional wages. The huge people's communes were put to work building dams and on irrigation projects, and thousands of workers were transferred from the cities to fill in planting and harvesting crops. Mao went to the countryside to cheer the program on: "Three years of suffering and a thousand years of happiness!" he promised.

In 1958, emboldened by Khrushchev's criticism of the Great Leap Forward, Peng Dehuai, who was now minister of defense, formed an open faction against Mao in the politburo. At the Eighth Congress of the CCP that summer, Peng won the election of his candidate, Liu Shaoqi, as president. Mao remained chairman of the CCP, but that position had become merely symbolic. Mao exploded with rage. He called the anti-Mao faction "capitalist roaders" and "women with bound feet" and departed for a vacation in Hangkow. He stayed in a house at the foot of a mountain, visited communes, and calmed down by taking long walks.

By 1959 it was evident that the Great Leap Forward was not going to be successful. Crop failures and mismanagement caused serious problems in China. To make matters worse, the Soviet Union publicly called the Great Leap Forward "the Maoist cavalry-charge approach to economic growth." In September, Khrushchev met with Mao in Beijing. The two reached no agreement and never met again. Soviet technicians and financial aid were withdrawn from China.

As it became clear that reports on successes of the Great Leap Forward had been exaggerated, the CCP leadership became more openly critical of Mao. Mao, however, had become more stubborn with advancing age and refused to modify his plan. If the communes were disbanded, he threatened, "I will go to the countryside to lead the peasants to overthrow the government. If those of you in the Liberation Army won't follow me, then I will go and find a Red Army, and organize another Liberation Army." He chastised his startled comrades: "Let the peasants and workers become the masters of their own destiny and they will produce. . . . The Communes came out of an earthshaking mass movement — and despite the problems and hardships that came with them, they are a gateway to a better future."

Mao at an international physicists' convention in Beijing in the mid-1960s. While Mao publicly downplayed the significance of nuclear weapons, he committed money and resources to China's development of an atomic bomb. The first Chinese nuclear device was detonated in 1964.

By 1960, however, it was plain that the experiment was an economic disaster. While the peasants struggled at their backyard blast furnaces, grain output fell. For the first time under the Communists, there was widespread hunger in the countryside. In the cities, a black market flourished. Mao continued to defend the Great Leap Forward. Peng was replaced as defense minister by Lin Biao.

Despite the failure of the Great Leap Forward, the Chinese masses trusted and loved Mao. At each anniversary of the Revolution, hundreds of thousands came into central Beijing's Tienanmen Square to see him stand and wave.

By early 1962, though, a full-scale depression with massive unemployment could not be ignored. Jobless workers were quickly sent to the countryside to work on communes. Others left for jobs in Hong Kong. *Newsweek* reported that there was widespread hunger in China, but not outright famine as in prerevolutionary times.

Mao with the Dalai (right) and Panchen (left) lamas, religious and national leaders of Tibet. Although Mao styled China as the enemy of imperialism and supporter of worldwide liberation movements, China took control of Tibet in 1950 and over the next 10 years imposed harsh constraints.

In late 1962 Mao began to hint that the Soviet Union was no longer socialist. It "has been usurped by revisionists," he declared. By 1964 the Soviet Union had become, in Mao's words, "a dictatorship of the bourgeoisie, a fascist German dictatorship and a Hitlerite dictatorship." In the winter of 1964–65, Mao asserted that he preferred the United States to the Soviet Union. The CCP politburo was shocked at Mao's extremist statements, but the Chinese masses enjoyed his outbursts of independence. He began to make emotional speeches aimed at people struggling for independence and equality in other countries. He attacked racism in the United States and announced his support for black Americans struggling for racial equality. China became a rallying point for anticolonial struggles around the world. Third World nations began fighting for the People's Republic of China's admission to the UN. (The Nationalist government on Taiwan was seated in the UN as the representative of the Chinese people.) Zhou Enlai traveled to Africa to meet with revolutionary leaders.

Despite the Soviets' refusal to help, efforts to build an atomic bomb had progressed in China. A Chinese scientist working in the United States, Qian Xuesen, had been harassed by anticommunists in that country and was deported in 1955. When he returned to China, he was given leadership of a team of scientists to build the first Chinese nuclear bomb. In the fall of 1964, China exploded its first nuclear device. The news spread over China and the world. Mao's popularity soared again. He announced that China would build only a few more bombs. His aim was to "break the monopoly of the two superpowers." In the Soviet Union, Khrushchev had been replaced by Alexei Kosygin and Leonid Brezhnev; in the United States, Lyndon Johnson was now president. CCP leaders urged Mao to make peace overtures to the two new leaders. Mao fought the proposal bitterly. By 1965 the United States was sending troops to aid South Vietnam in its war against North Vietnam and communist guerrillas. Convinced that war was a strong possibility,

Students waving *Quotations from Chairman Mao*, the famed "little red book," surround Mao and his defense minister, Lin Biao, in September 1966. As opponents sought to edge Mao from power, he used the loyalty of the armed forces and the students to launch a new revolutionary movement.

Mao evacuated children from the cities and called Liu and his supporters "deviationist intellectuals."

Soviet economic planning methods gradually revived the Chinese economy. Steel production soared, and new low-rent housing, health clinics, and nursery schools were built. The CCP leadership had not persuaded Mao to criticize himself, so they went around him, making decisions behind his back. "They treated me like a dead ancestor," Mao commented later. The Chinese people lavished praise on Mao for their improved standard of living, but even this did not help his spirits.

In May 1964 a little red-covered book called *Quotations from Chairman Mao* was published by the political department of the PLA. Hundreds of thousands of copies were sold or distributed within weeks. Lin Biao had started a massive reform of the PLA in 1964. All military ranks were abolished, and officers were ordered to work in the countryside or in factories for one month out of every year. The "thought of Mao Zedong" was an important part of the training program for new recruits. While the party treated Mao "like a dead ancestor," the PLA treated him like a living saint.

Mao and Liu Shaoqi (to Mao's left), his chief rival within the CCP, review a huge demonstration in Beijing to protest U.S. involvement in the Vietnam War. The presence of U.S. troops in Vietnam and the continued deterioration of relations with the Soviet Union left Mao concerned that the United States and the Soviet Union were acting together to isolate China.

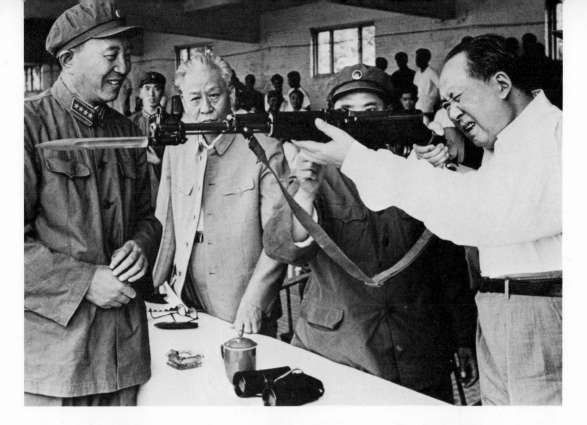

In the winter of 1965, Mao revisited Jinggang-shan. Memories of the early days of the Revolution made him bitter. When he came back to Beijing, he made sarcastic remarks at party meetings. "These days a Party branch secretary can be bribed with a few packs of cigarettes, and by marrying a daughter off to a cadre there's no telling what you can get as a reward. There are at least two factions in our Party. The socialist faction and the capitalist faction."

Most people thought Mao was referring to Liu Shaoqi, who lived in a luxurious home with a fashionable wife. He had written his own book, *How to Be a Good Communist*, and it had become a best seller. When Liu opposed Mao's proposals for a socialist education movement in the countryside, Mao lashed out at him: "The key point of this movement is to rectify those people in positions of authority within the party who are taking the capitalist road." The rage in Mao's voice made it clear that he had decided to get rid of Liu, but people had no way of guessing that the idea hatched at Jinggangshan went much farther than that.

Mao examines a rifle at a military exhibition in 1964. In the early 1960s, as Mao's authority was challenged by Liu Shaoqi (second from left), he was still able to count on the loyalty of the People's Liberation Army (PLA), as the Red Army was now known.

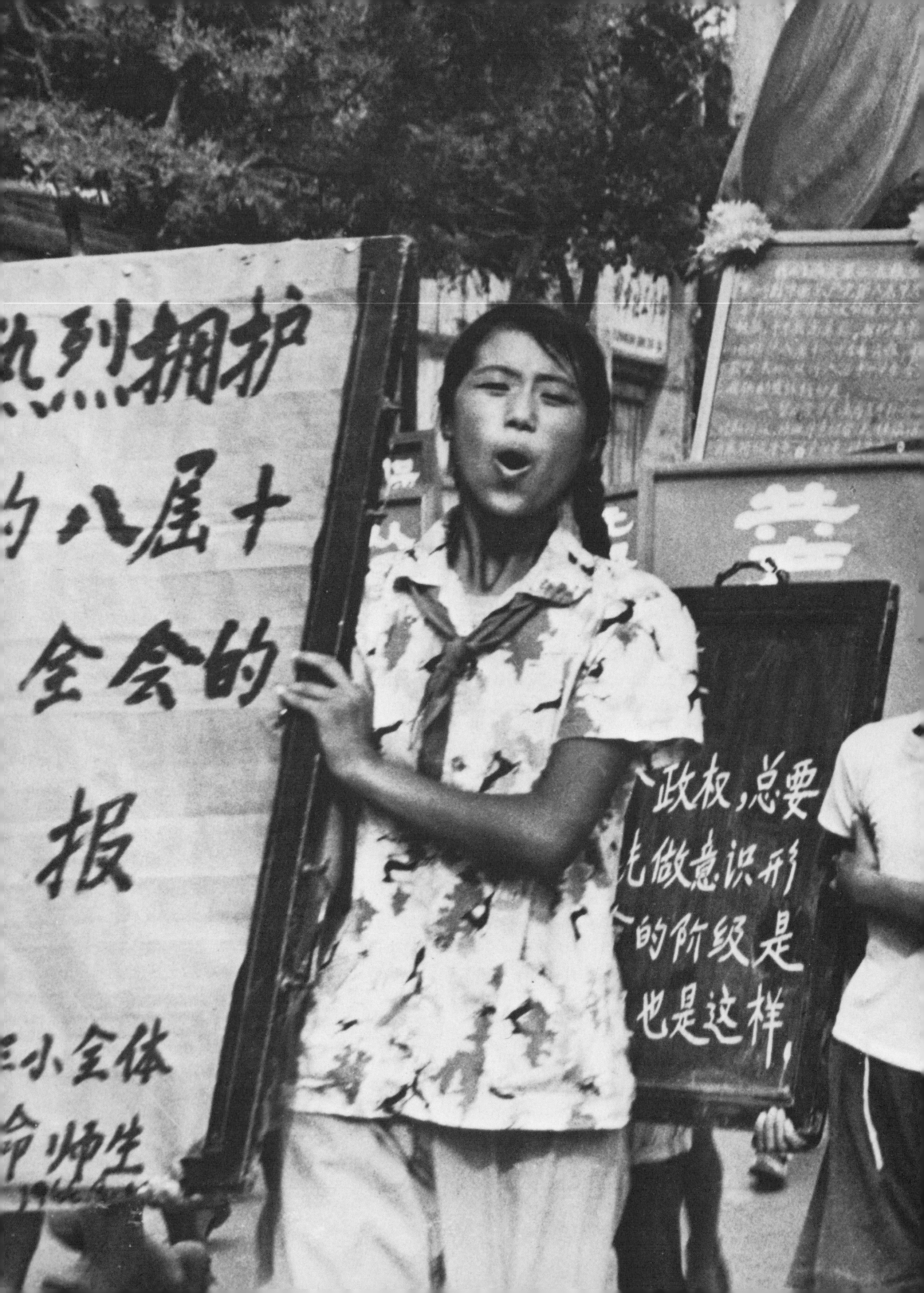
烈拥护
八届十
全会的
报
小全体
师生
政权，总要
做意识形
的阶级是
也是这样，

9

The Last Battle

Mao and Jiang Qing spent the fall and winter of 1965 in Shanghai, recruiting dissident intellectuals for a campaign that Mao had decided to initiate, a revolution on the political, ideological, and cultural fronts. The CCP leadership had, in Mao's opinion, reduced socialist ideals to a lust for consumer goods and had turned their backs on Mao's proposals. The party leadership had grown complacent, and the party itself had grown bourgeois and counterrevolutionary. The 300 million Chinese youth born since 1949 were too soft, Mao felt. A war of their own would toughen them up.

Mao intended to use the PLA and his friends among the intellectuals to launch a giant children's crusade against the bureaucracy, including the top party organizations. The spirit of the Chinese Revolution would be revived, the "capitalist roader" leaders of the CCP would be dethroned, and Mao would be head of the revolution again. The projected transformation would be called the Great Proletarian Cultural Revolution.

[No] modern statesman brought such profound and pervasive change to so many millions of people within so short a span of history.
—STANLEY KARNOW
American writer, on Mao

Students carry placards with slogans supporting Mao during the Great Proletarian Cultural Revolution, launched by Mao in 1966 to restore his own influence and the revolutionary ardor that had carried the Communists to power. In the turmoil that followed, Mao eliminated his opponents, including Liu Shaoqi.

Jiang Qing (left) and Zhou Enlai (center) address a rally of Red Guards, specially trained young supporters of Mao, in Beijing in August 1966. Jiang Qing supported the cultural revolution, seeking to impose ideological conformity on the arts. Zhou outwardly supported the revolution while working to restrain its excesses.

First, Jiang began a radio campaign to bring the arts in line with Maoist thought. She denounced all things Western: jazz and rock music, impressionist and abstract painting, Western-style clothing. Then, in February 1966, Mao ordered thousands of high-school and college students to leave school and work in communes. Universities were shut down and turned into centers for mass meetings, called people's communes. A month later, a wall poster went up in Beijing, signed by Lin Biao and Mao, announcing that the mayor and the entire city council were fired and had been replaced by a people's commune. Six million high-school and college students were organized into two new organizations: the Red Guards and the Young Pioneers. Lin Biao announced that their purpose would be to ensure "the protection of Chairman Mao and his teachings from Chinese reactionaries."

Liu Shaoqi, who was now president of the party, called an emergency meeting and proposed the disbanding of the Red Guards and Mao's resignation as party chairman. Liu lost the vote by a slim margin. The PLA was solidly behind Mao's plan. Liu remained president, but Lin Biao, as defense minister, held the real power.

In July Mao swam nine miles in the Yangzi River to refute rumors that he was too old and too ill to make decisions. On August 18, 1966, at a huge rally in Beijing, it was announced that schools would remain shut for four months. The Red Guards, now 14 million strong, were ordered to spread all over China to eliminate all who opposed the "thought of Chairman Mao," to turn China into a "great school," and to turn each man and woman into a true Communist.

Soon Red Guards were racing through the cities, pasting posters on walls and buildings, and criticizing officials, teachers, and factory foremen. Liu Shaoqi was put under house arrest. Anyone who had opposed the Great Leap Forward was suspect. As the campaign mounted, it became a reign of terror. Shops and museums were raided, and Western clothing and art treasures were burned in public squares. Anything connected with "Old China" or "Western ways" was a target for confiscation or destruction — temples, sunglasses, chess sets, and books from the West. The PLA transported the students, fed them, and protected them from arrest or reprisal.

The world press was near unanimous in its criticisms. The Great Proletarian Cultural Revolution was portrayed as a giant witch-hunt, but Mao had achieved his goal: The CCP had been cleansed of

Mao reviews crowds in Beijing. One result of the cultural revolution was the virtual deification of Mao. He was revered as the "Great Helmsman" of the revolution, and his opponents were attacked by the Red Guards as "capitalist roaders" and "deviationists."

A U.S. soldier in Vietnam. The increased U.S. involvement in the war and the easing of tension between the United States and the Soviet Union were factors in Mao's decision to normalize relations with the United States.

Mao's opponents, and all key party positions were now held by his supporters. New paintings and statues of Mao appeared everywhere. Mao's "Little Red Book" became China's bible. Engineers, mathematicians, and Ping-Pong players credited their successes to Mao's writings. Most of the Red Guards returned to school, and the PLA stood guard all over the nation, defending the Mao cult.

In the summer of 1967, thousands of Red Guards decided to go back to the cities when school let out to continue the Cultural Revolution. This time foreign diplomats became the prime targets. Moscow had to airlift the families of Soviet diplomats out of Beijing to save them from rampaging mobs. When the Red Guards marched on the British Mission, burned it to the ground, and forced its occupants to bow before a giant photo of Mao, things seemed to be getting out of hand, even in Mao's opinion. When Shanghai students took over the government there and proclaimed a commune, Mao called them anarchists and ordered them to disband. He left Beijing and traveled to various spots. Disturbed by the Red Guards fighting among themselves and attacking industrial workers, he ordered the schools to reopen and the students to return to school or to work on communes.

It was not easy to stem the tide of rebellion once it had started. Finally Mao had to use the PLA to call off his dogs. The soldiers were instructed to arrest anyone who continued to destroy property. He told a group of students that they could not treat all of China's adults like landlords.

At the Ninth Congress of the CCP, in 1969, PLA uniforms were worn by more than half the delegates. Mao was beginning to wonder if the PLA had too big a role in Chinese politics. Everyone had assumed that Mao, now a tired 74 year old, would name Lin as his successor, but he hesitated to do so.

The Americans, however, were having their own problems. Despite his aggressive policies in Vietnam, where he had expanded the war by invading Cambodia and Laos, U.S. president Richard Nixon was making speeches saying that he wanted to "pull China back into the family of nations." Zhou Enlai urged Mao to soften his foreign policy. Tension between China and the Soviet Union erupted into war along the China-Soviet border in 1969. With Nixon's top foreign-policy adviser, Henry Kissinger, pushing a policy of détente — an easing of tension between the United States and the Soviet Union — Mao feared the consequences of an alliance between those two nations.

Lin and many PLA officers regarded the United States as China's foremost enemy. At a central committee meeting in the fall of 1970, Lin and his generals opposed any overtures to Nixon. No official decision was reached, but Mao had decided. At National Day celebrations in October, Mao gave a brief speech about the friendship of the American people and invited his American journalist friends Edgar and Lois Snow to stand on the balcony beside him as he waved to the crowds. He told Snow that Nixon would be welcome to visit China.

Within a few weeks, Mao's latest initiatives were making headlines around the world. Mao Zedong had called for peaceful coexistence between the United States and China; he had returned 27 Chinese ambassadors to their overseas posts. Anxious for peace and also for trade agreements, Canada, France, and Italy all recognized the People's Republic of China and began pressing for its admission to the UN.

Zhou Enlai and U.S. president Richard Nixon at the welcoming banquet for Nixon in Beijing in 1972. Nixon's trip to China was the first time a U.S. president had visited that country. Mao was in poor health at the time and met only briefly with Nixon.

Mao with Deng Xiaoping, who emerged from the Cultural Revolution as Mao's heir apparent in 1973, only to be toppled again by the unpredictable Mao. The resilient Deng became China's leader after Mao's death in September 1976.

In 1971 Zhou Enlai gave the Chinese national Ping-Pong team permission to participate in the world championship matches in Tokyo, Japan. As the Chinese team was about to leave Tokyo for home, they invited the American team and some American newsmen to tour China. It was the first time an American group had been invited to China since 1949. Nixon made the next move, easing a 21-year U.S. trade embargo and allowing Americans to visit China for the first time without risking the loss of their passports.

Mao went ahead with plans for U.S. secretary of state Henry Kissinger to visit China to pave the way for a Nixon-Mao meeting. Lin Biao reacted by intensifying his opposition to Mao's new policy. Mao moved swiftly and fired the generals closest to Lin, claiming that he was protecting his old friend from a plot. Kissinger made a secret visit to Beijing to see Zhou, and on July 15, 1971, Nixon announced that he would go to China.

Lin and his associates were not about to relinquish their status so easily, however. They reportedly schemed to overthrow Mao, even to assassinate him. Mao learned of the plot, however, and Lin attempted to flee to Moscow. His plane crashed over Manchuria, however, killing Lin and all aboard.

The last stumbling block to a U.S.-China summit had been removed. In February 1972, Richard Nixon arrived in Beijing. He and Mao exchanged greetings and insignificant pleasantries through their interpreters. Nixon was then whisked away by limousine to the Great Hall of the People, where the best chefs in China had prepared an impressive banquet. Mao did not join the feast. He turned the negotiations over to Zhou and heard a report on the proceedings each evening.

Nixon, who years before had been called the "God of Plague and War" in the Chinese press and who had repeatedly worked to block China's admission to the UN, stayed in China for an unprecedented eight days. One of America's foremost opponents of Communist China was photographed smiling happily on the Great Wall, built many centuries earlier to protect China from foreign invasion. By the time Zhou saw Nixon off in Shanghai, the results of the summit were known. The United States would as-

Mao named Hua Guofeng (right, with outstretched hand) to succeed Zhou Enlai as premier after Zhou's death in January 1976. Hua's election was a compromise between more conservative factions and the leftist wing, led by Jiang Qing.

China after Mao still has many problems to solve. Foremost among them is the country's enormous population, estimated in the late 1980s to be approaching 1 billion. Deng's government advises young people to delay marriage, and couples are discouraged from having more than one child.

sume a lower profile in the dispute between China and Taiwan. There would be cultural exchanges and, later, a resumption of trade and diplomatic relations between the United States and China.

It was no longer possible for Mao to cover up the signs of his advancing age and illness. His tremors, which had begun in the mid-1960s, worsened. He was never again to appear in public. Meanwhile, Mao's opponents in the CCP leadership worked around him. Officials dismissed during the Cultural Revolution were restored to their jobs, discipline returned to the universities, and material incentives were reintroduced in industry.

In 1973 Mao seemed to revive a little. China had at last been admitted to the UN, and leaders of many nations came to pay their respects to the aged Mao for the first time. At a banquet for Prince Sihanouk of Cambodia, guests were shocked to see Deng Xiaoping, whom Mao had banished for six years as a "capitalist roader," sitting at the main banquet table. Zhou, who was now dying of cancer, had arranged Deng's restoration to favor, getting him to write a letter to the central committee expressing his outrage at Lin Biao's treason. Mao decided to forgive Deng and then shocked everyone by appointing him as vice premier.

By this time, the favorite sport in Beijing was guessing whom Mao would appoint to succeed him. Zhou was too old and too ill; Jiang Qing clearly wanted to be the new empress; and Hua Guofeng, Mao's protégé from Hunan, lacked experience. In 1974 Zhou entered a hospital in Beijing, and Mao went south for eight months. It was clear that they were no longer running China: Jiang Qing stayed in Beijing while Mao vacationed. She had been making statements to the press for months about the virtues of women in government, and Mao had grown angry at her none-too-subtle demonstration of high ambition. When Mao returned to Beijing, he stayed away from party meetings. He appeared to trust no one, least of all his wife.

Zhou Enlai died in 1976. His death stimulated further scrambling for power. Zhou had wanted

Mao to select Deng as premier, but Deng supported the reversal of the educational reforms of the Cultural Revolution, and Mao released an angry statement to the press, with Deng his obvious target. It now became clear that Mao had chosen Hua Guofeng as his successor. The educational issue had served as a pretext for Mao's demoting Deng in order to promote Hua, who was then elected to the top politburo position.

Doctors were constantly in attendance on Mao at this time, and visitors were kept out. The entire politburo met at Mao's bedside in the middle of the summer. By August he lay in a coma, and on September 9, 1976, at age 83, Mao Zedong was pronounced dead. A week of mourning was announced, and Mao's body was placed for public viewing in the Great Hall of the People.

Shortly before his death, in a press release aimed at Deng, Mao had written his predictions of China's future. "Perhaps the Right Wing will seize power after my death," he wrote. "If the Right Wing seizes power, it will be able to use my words to retain power for a time. But the Left will use other quotations of mine, and organize themselves, and overthrow the Right Wing. You are making the socialist revolution, and yet you don't know where the bourgeoisie is. It is right in the Communist Party — those in power taking the capitalist road."

Even Mao's predictions fell short of the mark. Hua Guofeng was easily won over to the cause of those who had opposed Mao in the CCP leadership. Mao's wife and three senior party members who had come to prominence during the Cultural Revolution — called "the Gang of Four" by the rest of the politburo — were accused of plotting to seize power, put on trial, expelled from the party, and denounced as ultrarightists and counterrevolutionaries. Soon after, Deng emerged as the nation's leader.

Many of Mao's policies have been reversed since his death, but the new leadership has proven reluctant to make a full-scale effort to destroy his legacy. He remains the sacred father of the Chinese Revolution.

Mao's portrait hangs over Tienanmen Square, the entrance to the Forbidden City in Beijing. In the mid-1980s China's leaders acknowledged that Mao erred during the Cultural Revolution, but he remains the dominant figure in modern Chinese history.

Further Reading

Archer, Jules. *Mao Tse Tung.* New York: Hawthorn, 1972.

Hsu, Immanuel C.Y. *The Rise of Modern China.* 3rd ed. New York: Oxford University Press, 1983.

Rejai, M., ed. *Mao Tse-tung on Revolution and War.* Garden City, NY: Doubleday, 1970.

Ruis and Friends. *Mao for Beginners.* New York: Random House, 1980.

Schram, Stuart. *Mao Tse-tung.* New York: Simon & Schuster, 1986.

Snow, Edgar. *Red Star Over China.* New York: Random House, 1938.

Terrill, Ross. *Mao: A Biography.* New York: Harper & Row, 1980.

Wilson, Dick. *The People's Emperor Mao.* Garden City, NY: Doubleday, 1980.

Chronology

Dec. 26, 1893	Born Mao Zedong in Shaoshan, Hunan Province, China
Oct. 1911	Joins Sun Yat-sen's revolutionary army
1917	Founds New People's Study Society
1918	First encounters Marxism
1919	Organizes United Students Association of Hunan; joins delegation to Beijing
1920	Organizes Marxist groups in Changsha and establishes radical bookstore
July 1921	Helps found Chinese Communist party (CCP) in Changsha
1921–1924	Organizes trade unions in Changsha; begins Hunan branch of CCP
	Guomindang and CCP unity agreement
March 1925	Death of Sun Yat-sen
April 1927	Chiang Kai-shek outlaws CCP, ending united front
Oct. 1928	Chiang establishes national government at Nanjing
1928	Mao organizes First Workers' and Peasants' Revolutionary Army; leads Autumn Harvest Uprising in Hunan
1928–1929	Reorganizes forces in Jinggangshan; establishes soviets in Hunan and Jiangxi
1930–1934	Resists Chiang's extermination campaigns
Oct. 1934–Oct. 1935	Long March
July 1937	Full-scale Japanese invasion of China
Dec. 1941	World War II begins in Asia
1942–1944	U.S. emissaries encourage Guomindang and CCP to unite against Japan
Aug. 1945	United States drops atomic bombs on Japan, ending World War II; Mao and Chiang agree to a temporary cease-fire
1946–1949	Civil war in China ends in victory for Mao's forces
Oct. 1, 1949	Mao proclaims the People's Republic of China
Jan. 2, 1950	Meets with Stalin in Moscow
Oct. 1, 1950	China enters Korean War
1952	First Five-Year plan implemented
March 1953	Policy of peaceful coexistence with Soviet Union begins
1957	"Hundred Flowers" campaign in China
1958–1960	Great Leap Forward
1964	China explodes its first atomic bomb
1966	Great Proletarian Cultural Revolution begins
June 1967	China tests its first hydrogen bomb
Feb. 1972	U.S. president Richard Nixon visits China
Jan. 8, 1976	Death of Zhou Enlai
Sept. 9, 1976	Mao dies in Beijing

Index

Hedda Garza lives in upstate New York where she works as a free-lance writer, editor, and lecturer. Her articles have appeared in several national magazines and her *Watergate Investigation Index* won the best academic book award from *Choice* magazine. She is also the author of *Trotsky* and *Franco* in the Chelsea House series *World Leaders   Past & Present*.

Arthur M. Schlesinger, jr., taught history at Harvard for many years and is currently Albert Schweitzer Professor of the Humanities at City University of New York. He is the author of numerous highly praised works in American history and has twice been awarded the Pulitzer Prize. He served in the White House as special assistant to Presidents Kennedy and Johnson.

PICTURE CREDITS

Acme Newspictures: p. 50; The Bettmann Archive: pp. 2, 15–17, 19, 24, 29, 72, 104; China Photo Service: p. 22; Culver Pictures, Inc.: pp. 39, 66, 71, 74, 76, 77; Eastfoto: pp. 14, 27, 34, 38, 42, 54, 56, 58, 60–62, 65, 69, 73, 79, 80, 86, 88, 92, 93, 95–97, 100, 101, 105; New China Pictures: p. 63; Snark International: p. 31; Sovfoto: pp. 32, 33, 45, 85, 90; Gary Tong: p. 64; UPI: pp. 59, 68, 78, 98, 102; UPI/Acme: p. 70; UPI/Bettmann Newsphotos: pp. 40, 51, 53, 75, 84, 94, 103, 106, 107; Xinhua News Agency: pp. 12, 26, 28, 36, 37, 46, 48, 52, 82